TABLE
MOUNTAIN
WALKS

*This book is dedicated with admiration and respect to
Professor W P U Jackson who loves Table Mountain and its
flowers and who knows so much more about them than I do.*

D0293807

TABLE
MOUNTAIN
WALKS

Colin Paterson-Jones

STRUIK

AUTHOR'S ACKNOWLEDGEMENTS

I should like to thank: Paul Britton of Cape Town Municipality's Parks and Forests Branch who made available his department's maps of the paths on the Table Mountain chain and who freely gave valuable advice on the routes. Howard Langley, Chief Nature Conservation Officer of the Western Cape Regional Services Council and his staff at the Cape of Good Hope Nature Reserve, in particular Jim Hallinan, for information on the reserve and its fauna. Pam Eloff who drew the maps for this book and who walked the routes independently herself, no mean feat in the time available. Marje Hemp, project editor, for her unfailing patience and her kind guidance. Dianne Stafford who typed the text accurately from my atrociously untidy handwritten draft. And, in particular, my wife Dee whose support, encouragement, critical advice and professional knowledge, she has given unstintingly as ever.

PUBLISHER'S NOTE

While every effort has been made to ensure that the text and maps are accurate and the routes described are safe, neither the author nor the publisher nor the cartographer will accept responsibility for any damages resulting from the use of this book.

PREVIOUS PAGE: *An early morning view of the eastern face Mountain from Silvermine.*
OVERLEAF: *Table Mountain, flanked by Devil's Peak and Lion's Head, is a sight that has excited generations of seafarers.*

Struik Publishers
(a member of The Struik Group)
80 McKenzie Street
Cape Town
8001

Reg No.: 63/00203/07

First published 1991

Copyright text and photographs © Colin Paterson-Jones
Copyright maps © Pam Eloff

Project editor: Marje Hemp
Copy editor: Jan Schaafsma
Cover and concept design: Abdul Amien
House designer: Petal Palmer

DTP make-up by Struik DTP, Suzanne Fortescue
Reproduction by: Unifoto (Pty) Ltd, Cape Town
Printed and bound by: Kyodo Printing Co (Singapore) Pte Ltd

ISBN 1 86825 181 0

Contents

ABOUT THIS BOOK

This book is an introduction to the pleasure, stimulation and tranquillity that walking in the mountains of the Cape Peninsula provides. It is organised into five chapters in which are described walks from a common starting point or walks in a naturally defined area. An essential feature of all these walks is that they require no rock climbing and offer no exposure to high drops.

For each walk there is a detailed map of the route showing contours and other salient features along the way, a summary and a detailed description which includes interesting points of natural or historical interest. The summary includes the total walking time for the route, an indication of the physical exertion required, an estimation to the nearest 50 m of the cumulative height climbed along the route, a description of the starting point, a route summary with times for the separate stages, possible route options and how the walk can be combined with other walks, and a description of any places which walkers may find difficult.

The times quoted are for steady walking by a reasonably fit person and are consistent within the book; very fit walkers may well complete the routes much faster and the not-so-fit should allow extra time. The times given do *not* include any stops along the way.

At the time of writing, no entry permits were required for the areas traversed by the walks.

Table Mountain and the Peninsula are a walker's paradise with a vast network of paths, major and minor. The routes have been chosen to provide a reasonable coverage of the available areas and only paths which are recognised by the authorities administering the areas have been described.

A spectacular stand of Bulbinella nutans *var.* turfosicola *on Constantiaberg after a recent fire.*

INTRODUCTION

Dominated by the well-known outline of Table Mountain, Devil's Peak and Lion's Head, the Cape Peninsula mountain chain stretches 50 km southwards to Cape Point to form one of the most scenically attractive recreational areas in southern Africa. Here are magnificant views of hidden valleys, isolated landscapes, steep cliffs and the restless ocean waiting to be discovered by the enthusiastic hiker.

In addition the plant life of the Peninsula is varied, rich and beautiful. The present appearance of Table Mountain and the chain of mountains down the Peninsula reflects the geological processes which formed them, the effects of climate and weathering, the plants which grow on them and the impact that man has had, particularly during the last four centuries.

GEOLOGY AND TOPOLOGY

The rocks which make up these mountains are essentially of three types. They stand on a base of shale of the *Malmesbury series*, a very ancient sedimentary rock which, in weathered form, is evident in several places on the lower slopes as orange or red-brown clay soils. The hard, grey, crystalline *Cape granite* is obvious in the rounded shapes of the boulders which are exposed on Lion's Head and along the Twelve Apostles. This igneous rock was formed when magma infiltrated and penetrated the Malmesbury shales. The characteristic grey rock of the upper slopes and mountain tops is *Table Mountain sandstone*, a more recent sedimentary deposit onto Malmesbury shales and granite.

The present appearance of Table Mountain is the result of two processes. The buckling and uplifting of the originally horizontal sedimentary deposits about 250 million years ago gave rise to the characteristic fold mountains of the south-western Cape. Tilted strata are obvious in nearby ranges but in Table Mountain the strata remained essentially horizontal; weathering and erosion over tens of millions of years have carved its present form.

The relative hardness of Table Mountain sandstone is responsible for the steep, fissured cliffs on the east, north and west faces below the Front Table and along the Twelve Apostles which make up the series of buttresses separated

Weathered sandstone clearly shows its sedimentary origin.

by steep ravines which are characteristic of these faces. On the east face of Table Mountain they are Ascension Buttress, Protea Buttress, Fernwood Peak, Window Buttress and Castle Rock and, on the west, the Twelve Apostles.

The Front Table, which includes the highest point in the Peninsula, Maclear's Beacon (1 085 m), does not cover a large area. To the south, it falls away to the Back Table. This is split by Disa Stream which runs into Orange Kloof, a large kloof which separates the Twelve Apostles and the moun-

tains above Llandudno and Hout Bay from the continuation of the Peninsula chain through Constantiaberg (927 m), Noordhoek Peak (756 m), Chapman's Peak (592 m) and Steenberg (536 m). In turn the Fish Hoek/Noordhoek valley separates this area from the rest of the chain, which incorporates Simonsberg (570 m), Swartkop (678 m) and Klaasjagersberg (576 m), and, on the eastern side of the Cape of Good Hope Nature Reserve, Paulsberg (366 m) and Vasco da Gama Peak (262 m).

WEATHER AND CLIMATE

The climate of the Peninsula is controlled mainly by the interplay of two systems which combine to cause most rain to fall during the winter months. Throughout the year a succession of cold fronts travels from west to east in the southern oceans. In the summer months, Atlantic high-pressure systems with an anti-cyclonic wind flow are situated to the south. This tends to force the cold fronts south of the Cape and to cause strong south-easterly winds to blow after the relatively calm conditions which accompany the passage of a cold front just south of the continent. The well-known 'table cloth' on Table Mountain is formed when air, which has picked up moisture from False Bay, is forced up and over the mountain by a strong south-easter and the moisture precipitates as cloud because of cooling and the drop in pressure. On the front face, as the cloud falls, it meets drier, warmer air and the moisture dissolves.

As winter approaches, the Atlantic high-pressure systems move north, allowing cold fronts to cross the south-western Cape and penetrate inland to varying distances. A typical winter weather pattern starts with the approach of a cold front which causes strong and gusting north-westerly winds to blow; after a day or so low-level cloud is blown in and it starts to rain. As the front moves east, the wind changes to south-west, bringing in very cold air and causing characteristic showers or, on high ground, snowfalls. These conditions seldom last long, and as the front moves away from the Cape, the weather behind it clears to produce beautiful, still sunny winter days, often followed by an off-shore flow of warm berg winds which presage the approach of another cold front, so repeating the pattern. The most stable weather on the Peninsula is in autumn as

the Atlantic high-pressure system moves north, the south-easters moderate and the cold fronts pass by to the south.

Temperatures on the Peninsula are moderate, stabilised by the proximity of the sea, and particularly the cold Atlantic Ocean on the west coast. Snow rarely falls on the top of Table Mountain and frost is virtually unknown. During summer the south-easter brings in cool air from the South Atlantic to moderate summer temperatures.

Rainfall varies greatly over the Peninsula because of the presence of the mountains, but in general the western and northern slopes are dry, whereas the eastern slopes are wet. In summer, clouds caused by the south-east wind deposit considerable amounts of moisture in the form of mist. This is not measured conventionally, yet has a significant effect on the plant life (and walkers!).

The weather on the Peninsula can be highly changeable within the broad seasonal patterns outlined above. For example, cold fronts can cross the Peninsula in mid-summer, causing temperatures to drop by as much as 15-20 degrees Celsius in a few hours; within minutes dense cloud can form on what was initially a cloudless day. Walkers should also take into account the wind-chill factor which effectively lowers ambient temperatures when strong winds blow: add the effects of a strong wind to wet clothing and you have instant refrigeration. Many walkers are also not fully aware of the dehydrating effects the strong winds and high solar radiation have on the Peninsula in summer. It is therefore only sensible to be prepared for any weather, even on a sunny day, and to choose routes suited to the season and prevailing conditions.

LEFT: *The weather in the Cape Peninsula can be extremely variable and is often unpredictable. Here the 'table cloth' pours over Table Mountain in a gale-force south-easter, while all is still at the kramat on Signal Hill.*

11

FLORA OF THE CAPE PENINSULA

One of the most striking aspects of the Table Mountain chain is the beauty and diversity of the plant life. Many botanists in the 17th and 18th centuries, including Thunberg, Masson, Paterson and Burchell, collected specimens and wrote of its magnificent floral richness.

The Cape Peninsula is part of the Cape Floral Kingdom, the smallest of the world's six floristic kingdoms. Confined to the tip of southern Africa, it covers only 4 per cent of the area, yet it ranks in species richness and density with the other floral kingdoms, including the Boreal Floral Kingdom which occupies most of the Northern Hemisphere, an area thousands of times larger. There are over 2 600 species of indigenous plants in the Cape Peninsula, more than in Great Britain, and more than half of these are found on Table Mountain alone. Many of them are rare, and many found nowhere else.

The plant life of an area is a product of its soils, aspect and climate, the interaction with insects, birds and animals (particularly modern man) and fire. Apart from relic patches of indigenous forest in Orange Kloof, the kloofs of the western slopes, on the eastern slopes of Table Mountain and in the Kalk Bay mountains, Table Mountain and the mountains of the Peninsula chain are covered with fynbos.

Fynbos

This veld type is a community of plants characterised by the presence of plants of one or more of three families, namely the Restionaceae or Cape reeds found here in place of the grasses characteristic of other veld types; the Proteaceae or protea family; and the Ericaceae – the ericas or Cape heaths. The word 'fynbos' comes from the Dutch 'fijn bosch' used to describe the plants with narrow leaves which make up a large proportion of fynbos communities. Typical of these are the ericas.

The fynbos has some affinities with veld types elsewhere in the world, for example the heathlands of Australia and the macchia of the Mediterranean, but is unique. Most fynbos plant communities grow on very infertile soils to which they are uniquely adapted. These soils have played a major role in the evolution of fynbos plants.

The dry lower north and west slopes of Table Mountain support a fynbos in which ericas (*Erica baccans*), pincushions (*Leucospermum conocarpodendron* or Kreupelhout)

ABOVE: *Restios,* Brunia nodiflora *and* Leucadendron xanthoconus *form a typical fynbos mosaic on the slopes of Constantiaberg.*

and proteas (*Protea nitida* or Waboom) are prominent. Before these slopes were burnt so frequently, they also supported large populations of the Suikerbossie (*Protea repens*), the nectar of which was gathered from the cup-shaped flower heads to be used as a syrup. The Waboom (so-named because its wood was used to make the spokes of wagon wheels) and the Kreupelhout survived because of their thick, fire-resistant bark. The word 'kreupelhout' originated from the Dutch and came to mean firewood because

shrubs gathered for firewood frequently had bent or 'crippled' branches; *Leucospermum conocarpodendron* was also used extensively for firewood by the early Dutch settlers at the Cape and was known as Kreupelhoutboom or 'Firewood tree' which has contracted to Kreupelhout over time.

On the higher cliff ledges there is a variety of small plants including succulent types such as the Red crassula (*Crassula coccinea*). The Front Table is characterised by short restioid growth which gives way to the taller, more diverse wet fynbos of the Back Table and the eastern slopes. Within these broad types, local conditions of aspect, soil type, rainfall and water run-off are reflected in the make-up of

the plant cover. The Silver tree (*Leucadendron argenteum*), prominent on the southern slopes of Lion's Head and above Kirstenbosch, grows only on weathered granite soils.

The types of fynbos encountered on Table Mountain are more or less representative of the other Peninsula mountains. On the lowland flats of the Cape of Good Hope Nature Reserve there is a form of mountain fynbos which has disappeared elsewhere or is under severe pressure from urban spread, agriculture and invasion by alien acacias.

In places, the vegetation on the Peninsula has been entirely modified by man through the establishment of plantations or paddocks for grazing, such as those on Groote Schuur Estate. Lion's Head and Signal Hill have become grassy; on the driest parts of Signal Hill, Lion's Head and the lower western slopes of Table Mountain the veld cover is renosterveld, characterised by the presence of grasses rather than restios, the renosterbos (*Elytropappus rhinocerotis*) and the kapokbossie (*Eriocephalus africanus*). The Renosterbos was first described as such in the 1685 diary of Simon van der Stel who wrote that, in the Olifants River valley, renosterbos was very common and rhinos were usually found in amongst the bushes there.

On the coast are found vegetation types adapted to salt spray and high winds and, in places, alkaline marine sands – thickets of wind-clipped milkwood trees (*Sideroxylon inerme*) are characteristic.

Restios

Of all the plant families which make up the fynbos, the Cape reeds or restios are perhaps the most characteristic. While not the most showy of the Peninsula plants, some are amongst the most beautiful. Restios are dioecious, ie with separate male and female plants, and most often grow together in large numbers – their subdued colouring plays a major role in the appearance of the fynbos. There are over 80 species of the Restionaceae on the Peninsula: some of the more easily recognised are *Cannomois virgata* (Besemriet), which has bright green fronds like upright horses' tails and grows in small dense stands in moist areas; *Chondropetalum mucronatum*, which has stout stems and grows in marshy areas on Table Mountain; and the low-growing *Elegia filacea*, which grows in large numbers on the flats of Cape Point.

Ericas

If the restios provide the background texture of the fynbos landscape, ericas or Cape heaths provide patches of bright

WILD FLOWERS OF THE CAPE PENINSULA

Fynbos contains more species of plants per square metre than is found anywhere else in the world. Because they are so numerous, the flowering plants of the Peninsula are not easy to get to know. The only comprehensive listing, Adamson and Salters' *Flora of the Cape Peninsula*, is out of date. Good reference books, although by no means comprehensive, are Mary Maytham Kidd's *Cape Peninsula – South African Wild Flower Guide 3*, published by the Botanical Society of South Africa, and Professor W.P.U. Jackson's *Wild Flowers of Table Mountain*.

Erica abietina *var.* echiiflora

Leucospermum conocarpodendron ssp. viride

Penaea mucronata

Stilbe ericoides

Gladiolus monticola

Ixia dubia

Watsonia humilis

Liparia splendens, *Mountain dahlia*

Crassula coccinea, *Red Crassula*

colour, as some species grow together in great numbers. There are more than 100 species of erica on the Peninsula, not including the minor genera. *Erica curviflora* colours wet areas a soft red in early summer while, in the same season, *Erica empetrina*, a Peninsula endemic, is a dusky pink on the south slopes below the Back Table. The low-growing *Erica lutea* provides splashes of white in spring and on the eastern slopes of Steenberg there is a large population of *Erica urna-viridis* plants which produce curious sticky, green flowers *en masse* in spring. Not all ericas grow in masses. *Erica abietina*, which has red tubular flowers, is common and widespread on Table Mountain, but most often only a few plants are seen together.

Proteacae

The protea family provides some of the larger broad-leaved plants which are characteristic of the fynbos. The family includes proteas, *Leucospermum* (pincushions), leucadendrons, *Mimetes, Serruria,* and others such as the Wild almond (*Brabejum stellatifolium*), which forms Van Riebeeck's hedge at Kirstenbosch. The word 'protea' comes from the name of the Greek god Proteus who could change his form at will and refers to the extraordinary diversity of the plant forms in this family.

A sight quintessentially of the fynbos is the yellowing of the veld at certain times of the year as the leucadendrons flower. In winter, the intense colour of *Leucadendron laureolum* bushes in the Silvermine and Cape of Good Hope nature reserves is unique.

Some of the large shrubs of the fynbos are the Silver tree, the Waboom and the Kreupelhout which have already been mentioned. Of the others, *Mimetes fimbriifolius* is widespread on the Peninsula and is endemic; these stout shrubs are an integral part of the landscape on the Back Table, the mountains and hills further south and in the Cape of Good Hope Nature Reserve.

Not all the members of the Proteaceae on the Peninsula are large bushes, however. *Diastella divaricata* ssp *divaricata* is very common on the Muizenberg mountains and further south to Cape Point; it forms low mats 1-2 m in diameter and has small, oval leaves and small pink flowers. One of the only two pincushions which occur on the Peninsula, the typical species of *Leucospermum hypophyllocarpodendron* has trailing stems that lie flat on the sand in which it grows, and produce sweetly scented yellow flower heads in spring. *Protea acaulos* has underground stems, and only tufts of leaves and small flower heads appear above the surface.

Bulbous plants

Plants which grow from tubers, rhizomes, corms or bulbs include some of the most spectacular plants of the fynbos. Many of these are members of the Iridaceae family. Watsonias, aristeas, bobartias and *Chasmanthe* often grow in dense stands and put on striking shows, especially soon after fires. The blues of the aristeas ranging from the most delicate powder blue of *Aristea spiralis* to the dark navy blue of the tall-growing *Aristea major* are a conspicuous part of the fynbos in summer. Blue is also the colour of the babianas, flowering in profusion on Signal Hill in spring, and of some species of moraeas. The Painted ladies of the Peninsula (*Gladiolus debilis* and *Gladiolus carneus*) are still relatively common. *Gladiolus aureus*, a beautiful yellow species which used to grow in sandy areas in the south, is virtually extinct because of urban sprawl and invasion of its habitats by alien acacias. Ixias, most of which flower in spring, come in all colours – from the red and yellow colouring of *Ixia dubia*'s flowers to the delicate, pale blues of *Ixia polystachya*.

Species of the Amaryllidaceae are most often seen after fire. The March lily (*Amaryllis belladonna*) flowers in profusion after fire, otherwise only sporadically; the pink to deep red flowers of the Fire lily (*Cyrtanthus ventricosus*) are seen only directly after a fire in amongst the ashes; the April fool flower (*Haemanthus coccineus*) also appears in great profusion after a burn. The so-called Guernsey lily (*Nerine sarniensis*) flowers in autumn in several places on the Peninsula; there is an unusual pink form of this species which is found on Devil's Peak.

Fire stimulates the flowering of *Bulbinella nutans* var. *turfosicola*, a species of the Lily family; the sight of thousands of its creamy-white flower-heads in a recently burnt seepage slope is magnificent (*see page 8*). Another well-known member of this family is *Agapanthus africanus* with its dark blue flowers.

Other fynbos plants

Not all splashes of yellow in the fynbos landscape are provided by the leucadendrons; dense stands of *Aspalathus* and *Cyclopia*, species of the legume family, are brilliant yellow in early summer. *Psoralea* spp, tall plants with sprays of blue flowers, and the Mountain dahlia (*Liparia splendens*) carrying large orange pendulous flowers, are just a few of a large number of plants of this family on the Peninsula.

The daisy family is also well represented. *Euryops abrotanifolius*, a small but conspicuous shrub with yellow flowers in winter, is common along the Pipe Track and the northern slopes of Table Mountain and Devil's Peak. *Osmitopsis asteriscoides*, a straggly aromatic plant with white flowers, is a major component of the plant cover in wet sites. The most impressive members of this family must, though, be the everlastings. The white everlasting (*Helichrysum vestitum*) transforms the landscape of Cape Point when it flowers in summer; another everlasting of the mountain slopes, *Helichrysum speciosissimum*, deserves its specific name which means 'most beautiful'. The Rain daisy (*Dimorphotheca pluvialis*) with its large white flowers, is widespread in the early spring.

Pelargonium cucullatum is a conspicuous plant in the fynbos veld with its magenta-coloured flowers. This species of the Geraniaceae family is one used in hybridising to produce the range of 'geranium' garden plants available

Pelargonium cucullatum *flowers best a year or two after fire; old plants become sparse and leggy.*

today. It is at its best within a few years of a fire, growing sparse and leggy thereafter. *Pelargonium myrrhifolium*, a small plant of the dry western and northern slopes of Table Mountain, is another member of this genus.

Although some members of the Rutaceae family are striking plants (the China flower, *Adenandra uniflora*, for example), their contribution to the fynbos environment is more often smelt than seen immediately. The leaves of plants of *Agathosma*, *Coleonema* and other members of this family, which includes citrus, give off pungent scents when crushed, some pleasant, some not. The fresh, aromatic scent of buchu (*Agathosma* spp) is an integral part of the fynbos environment.

Some of the smallest flowering plants on the Peninsula are amongst the most beautiful. Species of *Lobelia* and sorrel (*Oxalis* spp) are numerous. On seepage slopes, the glands on the red leaves of the insectivorous Sundews (*Drosera* spp) gleam in the sun and set off their simple, pink flowers to perfection.

Plants confined to the fynbos

Several families of plants are endemic to the fynbos. On the Peninsula the Penaeaceae, is represented by *Saltera sarcocolla*, a fairly common plant on open, rocky mountain slopes. It has characteristic sticky, pink flowers at the end of stems that carry four rigid and straight rows of tightly clasping leaves along their length. *Penaea* spp are smaller plants with the same leaf arrangement and creamy flowers ageing to maroon. The Bruniaceae is another family confined to the fynbos. *Berzelia lanuginosa*, with leaves somewhat like those of an erica and clusters of small cream-coloured balls in flower, is a plant of wet areas. *Brunia nodiflora* (Stompies) looks much the same but occupies open mountainsides. The Stilbaceae is also represented; in Cape Point in winter the bright pink flower-spikes of *Stilbe ericoides* stand out in the veld.

Rare and endemic plants on the Peninsula

The Cape Peninsula also has over 150 species of rare and threatened plants. *Staavia dodii*, a member of the family Bruniaceae, is known only from one locality in the Cape of Good Hope Nature Reserve. A member of the family Proteaceae, *Leucadendron strobilinum*, grows on damp mountain slopes on the Peninsula, and nowhere else. Only a few plants of a form (var. *echiiflora*) of a widespread species of erica, *Erica abietina*, have ever been seen, growing in a limited area on the Saddle between Devil's Peak and Table Mountain. Another rare endemic is *Erica halicababa*, a robust shrub which grows on cliff ledges; its specific name alludes to the large creamy-green flowers which are supposed to look like English gooseberries. *Brachysiphon fuca-*

tus (Penaeaceae), a rare endemic of damp rocky slopes, is a compact bush covered with dark pink flowers in winter.

Plants to avoid

The Blister bush, *Peucedanum galbanum*, is a member of another large fynbos family, the Apiaceae. The skins of some people are sensitised to sunlight simply by brushing against the leaves of this plant, and subsequent exposure to the sun can develop severe blistering. As with most allergenic reactions, different individuals react more or less – I seem to be practically immune.

Another uncomfortable group of plants for hikers is the genus *Cliffortia* which is related to the rose. Unlike roses, however, these are not beautiful plants, and their spiky leaves can make climbing through the dense stands which they form a painful experience. Despite this, a species of Cliffortia (*Cliffortia ruscifolia*) is known as 'Climber's friend' because its firmly rooted stems can be reliably used as handholds and footholds by rock climbers.

The fynbos year

One of the delights of the fynbos is that, whatever the season, there is always something flowering. Although the veld in summer may look dry and uninteresting from afar, this is the flowering season for some of the most spectacular fynbos flowers, including disas (*see* page 120), aristeas in all shades of blue, agapanthus and watsonias (especially *Watsonia tabularis*, named after Table Mountain), and the brilliant red *Crassula coccinea*, to name but a few. Surprisingly, February, possibly the driest month of the year, is the month with the highest number of erica species flower-

The Blister bush, Peucedanum galbanum.

ing. In late summer, the April fool flowers (*Haemanthus sanguineus*) and March lilies (*Amaryllis belladonna*) put on a fine show. May is the month with the least number of species flowering, but this is compensated for by the beauty of the mild, still days which characterise this time of year. In autumn, many proteas begin to bloom, as do some *Oxalis* species. September, October and November are the months with the most plant species flowering.

NATURAL FOREST

Compared with the fynbos, the forests of Table Mountain and the Peninsula chain are – in terms of species richness – poor. Of the estimated 2 600 plant species on the Peninsula, there are less than 100 species of indigenous trees and only about 30 species of forest trees.

Before the European settlement of the Cape four centuries ago, large areas of Table Mountain were covered with Afromontane forest. On the western and northern slopes, these were confined to the damp kloofs, but on the eastern slopes below the cliff face and into the kloofs, and in Orange Kloof and the Hout Bay valley, there were extensive tracts of forest because of the high rainfall or run-off in these areas. Within 50 years most of the forest was gone, felled for timber and fuel for the new settlement.

Of all the plant communities on the Peninsula, the natural forest is the most easily and permanently damaged. The erosion that accompanies the removal of trees is rapid because there is no fast growth from seed or by resprouting of vegetation to provide plant cover. Because trees regenerate slowly, and the process is successful only under optimum conditions, the re-establishment of forests by natural means takes centuries, not years. Although fires do not generally penetrate forests, they do destroy the bushy growth on the forest margins, and the result is a retreat of the forest edge. The extensive burning of the fynbos on Table Mountain has also resulted in a great reduction in the extent of the natural forest.

Indigenous trees

Some of the most common and easily recognised forest trees are the following :

The Yellowwood (*Podocarpus latifolius*) has a characteristic blueish bloom to its young leaves. It is a tree of the deep forest, but is also found on the margins and, in some open situations, as a large, rounded shrub. The Wild peach (*Kiggelaria africana*) has leaves with toothed margins and depressions along the mid-rib on the underside, while the Stinkwood (*Ocotea bullata*) has characteristic depressions along the mid-rib of its entire leaves. The Cape beech (*Rapanea melanophloeos*) is a large tree with glossy green entire leaves with a purplish leaf stem, and the Turkey-berry (*Canthium inerme*) is a small tree with glossy entire leaves and spines. The Bastard saffronwood (*Cassine peragua*) has orange bark and leaves with toothed margins.

The Keurboom (*Virgilia oroboides*), unmistakable in early summer when the tree is covered in slightly scented, pink, pea-like flowers, is often a forest pioneer, establishing itself readily along watercourses and other suitable locations.

The *'butter-spoons' of* Cunonia capensis.

The Rooiels (*Cunonia capensis*) carries spikes of creamy-white flowers in summer as well as 'butter-spoons' – upright spade-shaped bracts which contain a soft, butter-like material around the new growth. This tree is also often found along streams. The Hard pear (*Olinia ventosa*) has leaves which are dark green and glossy above but paler below, with a prominent mid-rib.

BIRDS OF THE CAPE PENINSULA

The Peninsula provides a variety of habitats for birds, many of which have adapted to the built-up areas and the plantations of exotic trees. Of the remaining natural areas, the largest habitat is the open fynbos veld. The rocks and cliff-faces provide another extensive habitat, as does the long coastline; far more limited habitats are the remaining patches of natural forest, coastal scrub and freshwater vleis.

Open Fynbos

The Orangebreasted Sunbird is very common in all the fynbos areas; it is a fynbos endemic. The females are a rather dull grey-green, but the males, who characteristically spend a lot of time chasing or being chased by other males, have bright orange-yellow breasts with a violet band above and iridescent green heads. Their characteristic calls are a constant accompaniment to walks in the fynbos. Less frequently seen are the males of the larger Malachite Sunbird which assume their full iridescent green plumage only in the breeding season; the males, too, are aggressive towards other males. Almost as vocal as the

Orangebreasted Sunbird are the Cape Sugarbirds with their yellow under-tail coverts and, in the males, their long tails. In the winter breeding season the males have a typical undulating display flight during which they flap their tails and at the same time utter their very distinctive hoarse grating calls.

Also common are Grassbirds: pairs of these beautifully marked small birds spend most of their time fossicking in the bushes, but emerge from time to time for a song. This

The Cape Sugarbird, a noisy and conspicuous resident in proteaceous fynbos. The long tail indicates that this is a male.

pleasant warbling song, which usually ends with a plaintive whistle, often accompanies a walk up a mountain slope. Karoo Prinias can be mistaken for Grassbirds at first glimpse but are not as well marked, and their colouring is drab in contrast to the more colourful Grassbird. Another bird which spends most of its time below the fynbos

canopy is the Neddicky, a small brown bird with light blue-grey underparts.

Flocks of Cape Siskins, small, dull grey-yellow birds similar to canaries, often frequent burnt areas of fynbos to rob dehiscent leucadendron cones of their seeds. Few walkers have not been startled by the sudden panicked flight of a disturbed Cape Francolin; small flocks forage for seeds early in the day, then rest up concealed in the bush. Steppe Buzzards can often be seen hunting over the fynbos in summer.

Rocky Mountain Slopes and Cliffs
Redwinged Starlings are frequently to be seen feeding in the fynbos, their characteristic cinnamon wing patches evident in flight. They will, however, always return to a rocky outcrop. Pairs have an endearing habit of calling softly to each other, a sound quite distinct from their harsh alarm call. Beautifully marked and coloured, Ground Woodpeckers are most often seen in small groups on the rocky upper slopes of the mountains. Other birds which perch on rocks are the Cape Rock Thrush, Sentinel Rock Thrush and Familiar Chat. Superficially the thrushes seem similar but the blue-grey on the head of the male Sentinel Rock thrush extends below the neck to the chest.

Rock Pigeons are common enough in built-up areas where they have adapted so well to roosting on high window ledges that their droppings have become a cleaning problem, but they are also to be found in rocky areas. It is exciting to sit on a high rocky peak in summer and to hear the sound of Black or Alpine Swifts flying close by you at high speed, feeding on the wing. Rock Martins, unlike swifts, fly silently and slowly by comparison. Even more exciting is the sight of a majestic Black Eagle soaring above; there are several breeding pairs on the Peninsula. Surprisingly large at close quarters, the Whitenecked Raven also rides the thermals next to cliff faces in search of food – as does the Rock Kestrel, a smaller raptor which characteristically hovers while searching for prey.

Indigenous Forest
The Sombre Bulbul, which has an overall grey-green colouring altogether different from that of the Cape Bulbul, frequents the fringes of forests. It is rarely seen but has a characteristic loud whistling call 'willie, willie' which pinpoints its position. The forest edge is the habitat for a number of birds, many of which are not, at first, easily spotted. The markings of the Cape Batis blend beautifully

with the branches and dappled light of its home inside large bushes and dense trees. Rameron Pigeons also often forage high in trees, especially those in fruit.

The Olive Thrush, Southern Boubou and Cape Robin all prefer to fossick for food at or near ground level in the bushes. The secretive Knysna Warbler which inhabits dense vegetation on forest fringes is considered one of the finest songsters in the Cape Peninsula. Also to be seen at the edge of the forest is the Dusky Flycatcher, an altogether drab bird compared with its namesake, the Paradise Flycatcher, which is a colourful bird with a blue beak, dark head, grey-blue underparts and orange-brown tail.

As the song of the Nightingale heralds spring in Europe, the unmistakable call of the Piet-my-vrou (Redchested Cuckoo) means that summer has come to the Cape; this bird is seldom seen, as it frequents the highest branches of trees or deep forest. It mainly parasitises the nests of the Cape Robin.

Cape of Good Hope Nature Reserve
Many of the birds of the coastal fynbos are the same as those found elsewhere in the montane fynbos. Unlike the other sunbirds, however, the Lesser Doublecollared Sunbird prefers bushier vegetation to the open fynbos and is often to be seen next to coastal scrub in the Cape of Good Hope Nature Reserve; the Cape Bulbul, with its characteristic white eye ring, and the Cape White-eye, similarly marked, have the same preference.

Sirkelsvlei in the Cape of Good Hope Nature Reserve is the only natural body of inland water encountered on the walks described in this book. Surprisingly, it does not have a prolific bird population, although Egyptian and Spurwinged Geese, African Black Duck and more rarely, Yellow-billed Duck, are sometimes seen there. This is in stark contrast with other vleis on the Peninsula such as Rondevlei, which is a popular bird sanctuary. The highly leached and acidic sand derived from Table Mountain sandstone around Sirkelsvlei supports a nutrient-poor vegetation. This may be the reason for one of the stranger sights of Cape Point, where, along the west coast, pairs of Egyptian Geese are often to be seen on the rocks next to the sea, and even swimming in the waves. For a duck species which elsewhere is most commonly found on inland fresh waters, this is unusual behaviour. It is likely that pairs with breeding territories in the reserve are forced to feed at the coast to obtain enough nutrition.

The 40-km long coastline of the Cape of Good Hope

Nature Reserve is the temporary or permanent home of large numbers of many other kinds of birds. Most common are Kelp and Hartlaub's Gulls, Cape, Bank, Crowned and Whitebreasted Cormorants and, in the right season, several Tern species.

Pairs or small groups of African Black Oystercatchers can be seen on the rocks and sandy beaches of the west coast; the reserve provides a secure breeding place for this sensitive species as well as for the small Whitefronted Plover.

The Grassbird pauses in its busy quest for food in the undergrowth to perch on a plant and have a song.

A delightful sight is a flock of Avocets on the beach, their black and white markings and long, upturned beaks making them unmistakable.

There is a resident pair of African Fish Eagles in the reserve, and an occasional African Marsh Harrier, now a rare species in the Cape Peninsula.

MAMMALS

Because of the infertile soils on which it grows, fynbos does not support large numbers or a wide variety of animals. The vegetation on the lower shale slopes of Table Mountain and the surrounding flats did, however, once provide grazing for many kinds of larger mammals, but with the settlement of the Cape, these animals were rapidly exterminated together with their predators. Outside the Cape of Good Hope Nature Reserve, one does not often see wild mammals on the Peninsula. The most likely to be encountered are dassies (Rock hyrax) on rock outcrops or the ledges of the Front Table of Table Mountain, and the Cape grey mongoose, briefly glimpsed while on a foray through the fynbos. I have never seen any buck on Table Mountain or in the Silvermine Reserve, although grysbok may well be present. The largest predator is the lynx which occurs on Table Mountain and other Peninsula mountains, but is secretive and rarely seen. Genets are present too, but, being nocturnal animals, are also seldom encountered. The porcupine is another strictly nocturnal animal and all that walkers are likely to see of this large rodent is the occasional quill on a path.

Moles and mole-rats live permanently underground, but the surface trails of the Cape golden mole are sometimes seen on the mountain, and a walk over a sandy area undermined by Cape mole-rats will soon reveal their presence. Cape golden moles are true moles and are insectivorous. Mole-rats are rodents which eat the corms and bulbs of bulbous plants. Two species, the Common mole-rat and the Cape mole-rat transport the corms or bulbs to their nests; those which are not eaten sprout and grow some distance away from their original locality. The Mole-rats thus provide a means by which bulbous plants are dispersed in the veld to provide a better chance of survival. Another rodent encountered on walks in the Peninsula is the Striped mouse – a shy animal – more often heard rustling in a bush than seen. Quite the opposite in behaviour are the Chacma baboons, as those accustomed to humans can become quite fearless and are potentially dangerous. Many baboons have had to be destroyed.

Most of the alien Himalayan tahr herd which grew from a pair which escaped from the now defunct zoo on Rhodes Estate in the late 1930s, have been shot because of the damage they caused to vegetation on the rock ledges on Table Mountain's cliffs.

REPTILES AND AMPHIBIANS

The Koggelmannetjie, Agama atra.

Reptiles are commonly seen in a variety of habitats all over the Cape Peninsula especially during the summer. Lizards are perhaps the most obvious as several species have a habit of sunning themselves on rocks. The koggelmannetjie (*Agama atra*), which can be quite spectacularly coloured, takes its common name from the way it nods its head when nervous. Another plentiful lizard is the black *Cordylus cordylus*. Angulate tortoises are particularly common in the Cape of Good Hope Nature Reserve where several, ranging in size from 10-cm babies to 50-cm adults, can sometimes be seen in the space of a few minutes.

Far less frequently encountered are the snakes of the Peninsula. The one snake you may see is the Puff-adder; unlike other snakes it does not move away at the approach of people. This behaviour, the result of its habit of lying still and waiting for its prey, makes it the most dangerous snake for walkers. Although they appear sluggish, Puff-adders strike extremely fast and, not unreasonably, dislike being trodden on. It is sensible to watch where you put your feet, but even this is not foolproof. On the Upper Contour Path on Table Mountain one spring day, I was fortunate to step over, rather than on, a large Puff-adder which was very effectively camouflaged by restios lying across the path; while I did my best to remain airborne, it moved off into the bush. Puff-adders are rare on Table Mountain, but more common on the lower slopes of the mountains further south, and common at Cape Point.

Berg adders are very occasionally seen in rocky areas, but the only other two snakes which may be encountered, apart from small sand snakes and similar reptilian equivalents of avian LBJs (little brown jobs – a description for those nondescript birds one often sees), are the Cape cobra and the Mole snake. The Cape cobra will almost always move off at the approach of hikers, but may become more aggressive during the breeding season in spring. This very venomous snake is fairly common in the Cape of Good Hope Nature Reserve. Mole snakes, probably the largest snakes on the Peninsula, are not venomous. The boomslang is also highly poisonous and common but almost never seen because it is extremely timid.

Although humans have an instinctive fear of snakes, statistics prove that they present far, far less of a hazard to walkers than carelessness on the part of some walkers themselves. Beating a snake to a pulp out of fear or for any

The Cape river frog, Rana fuscigula, *is plentiful next to mountain pools.*

other reason is tantamount to shooting dassies; both play an essential ecological role.

The Cape river frog (*Rana fuscigula*) is plentiful next to streams and pools. It varies considerably in appearance, some frogs have an overall beige colour, while others are much darker, and some sport white stripes down their backs. Table Mountain has its own endemic frog, the Thumbed ghost frog (*Heleophryne rosei*), which has adapted to life in the swift-flowing streams in some kloofs, where it clings to the rocks with specially evolved suction pads around its mouth while feeding off the algae. This rarity is nocturnal and secretive, so you are unlikely to see it.

INSECTS AND SPIDERS

Amongst the 75-odd species of butterfly which occur on the Peninsula the Peninsula thestor (*Thestor obscurus*), a smallish butterfly with reddish-brown wings without distinctive markings, is endemic. The Protea scarlet (*Capys alphaeus*) used to be common on Table Mountain but, as a result of great reductions in the populations of proteas (for example *Protea repens* and *Protea grandiceps*) through too frequent burns, its numbers have diminished because the caterpillars which are its larval stage feed on protea buds. The caterpillars of a common butterfly, the Garden acraea (*Acraea horta*), favour the leaves of the forest tree, the Wild

peach (*Kiggelaria africana*), and can sometimes strip the tree. The larvae of another widespread species, the Christmas butterfly or Citrus swallowtail, feed on, amongst other things, the leaves of the Blister bush (*Peucedanum galbanum*). The Table Mountain beauty (*Meneris tulbaghia*) is abundant on Table Mountain at higher altitudes and is attracted particularly to red flowers. The sight of this beautiful butterfly pollinating the flower of a Red disa is one of the treats of summer.

The flower heads of proteas and pincushions provide food for a variety of beetles, amongst which are Protea

The striking colour of these CMR (Cape Mounted Rifles) beetles warn would-be predators that they are poisonous.

beetles (Cetoniid beetles) with an iridescent green colour to their wings and a red-brown fringe of hairs. Equally colourful are Blister beetles (*Mylabris* species) – black beetles with large yellow or red spots.

Bees of many different kinds are a common sight as they go about their work of pollinating flowers. The Cape of Good Hope Nature Reserve is one of the few places where pure strains of the relatively docile Cape honey bee (*Apis mellifera capensis*) still occur.

Ants in the fynbos play another important role in the reproduction of plants. Many fynbos plants have evolved a strategy for seed dispersal and protection; they produce seeds with a special attachment, an elaiosome, which contains a powerful chemical attractant to some ants. The seeds collected by the ants remain underground in the ants' nests where they find a protected environment in which to germinate without predation or damage by fire.

Of the many spiders on the Peninsula, two of the Orb web spiders are particularly noticeable. The *Argiope* species are easily identified as they have yellow and black abdomens and weave golden webs suspended between two low bushes. The more dowdy, grey-coloured *Cyrtophora* species produce impressive webs with 'suspension cables' that can span a distance of up to 3 or 4 metres.

MAN'S INFLUENCE

Man's effect on the flora and fauna and appearance of the Peninsula has been marked. The early European sailors who rounded the Cape called it 'the land of fire' because of the frequent burning of the veld by the nomadic Khoi

The cableway provides the easiest way up and down Table Mountain which can be useful in an emergency or if time is short.

in an effort to improve grazing for their stock and to stimulate the growth of edible bulbous plants. Within fifty years of the first European settlement at the Cape, some 90 per cent of the indigenous forest which once covered the eastern slopes of Table Mountain and the Hout Bay valley had been felled for use as fuel, building, or making furniture and wagons: the natural forest found there today is a small remnant. Recently, the forests have experienced a new threat with the influx of Xhosa people to the southwestern Cape; Assegai trees (*Curtisia dentata*) are being stripped of their bark for use in traditional medicine. Protea wood produced good charcoal, and as a result the tall protea cover of the lower slopes soon disappeared. Urban spread has all but eliminated the fynbos of the flats.

Cape lion, leopard, hyena and even black rhinoceros once roamed the Peninsula but now all are gone. Of the larger mammals, all that remain are the adaptable baboons and the reintroduced eland, red hartebeest, mountain zebra, vaal rhebok, steenbok, Cape grysbok and bontebok in the Cape of Good Hope Nature Reserve. Smaller animals like dassies and reptiles fared better, and are still seen.

Pines were planted on Table Mountain late last century to stabilise erosion, to provide a source of timber and in a mistaken belief that plantations would increase water collection and run-off. Because these are now recognised as invasive aliens, plantations and self-seeded trees outside plantations have mostly been removed from its land in the last few years by the Cape Town City Council. Plantations on the lower slopes belonging to the Department of Environment Affairs at Cecilia and Tokai, and to the Council at Newlands, still stand. The Stone pine, a non-invasive alien, is a familiar sight on the front face, at Rhodes Memorial and on Rhodes Estate. Rhodes Estate is maintained artificially by the Department of Public Works as grassland to support the buck and alien deer herds there.

The most prominent man-made landmarks on the front face of Table Mountain are the two cable stations. The cableway was opened in 1929 and has since carried over 8 million passengers; it is the easiest way to ascend Table Mountain, but the least rewarding.

On the slopes of Devil's Peak stand the ruins of three blockhouses built as fortifications at the end of the 18th

KIRSTENBOSCH

The National Botanic Gardens at Kirstenbosch are world famous not only because of their uniquely beautiful setting against the eastern side of Table Mountain, but also because they contain an enormous and comprehensive collection of the plants which form the Cape Floral Kingdom. These gardens were the first national botanic gardens in the world to grow and display indigenous plants and the spectacular result draws tens of thousands of visitors per year.

Formerly owned by Cecil John Rhodes who purchased the property in 1895 and bequeathed it to the nation after his death in 1902, Kirstenbosch is now administered by the National Botanical Institute. This statutory body's mission is to 'provide the facilities, knowledge and expertise to ensure the conservation, sustained use, appreciation and enjoyment of South Africa's exceptionally rich flora and vegetation'. The gardens, established in 1913, are only the immediately obvious evidence of a larger activity which includes extensive research, conservation and education.

century during the first British occupation of the Cape; the best preserved is the King's Blockhouse which stands above Rhodes Memorial. Prominent on the lower eastern slopes are Rhodes Memorial, the University of Cape Town's upper campus and the National Botanic Gardens at Kirstenbosch. On the Back Table are several dams; the two largest, Woodhead Reservoir and Hely-Hutchinson Reservoir, once supplied all of Cape Town's water requirements. Water was piped through the Woodhead Tunnel, down Slangolie Ravine and along the lower western slopes to a filtration plant above Kloof Nek.

The Silvermine Nature Reserve, which links the mountains to the east of Hout Bay and the Muizenberg mountains, is administered by the Cape Town City Council. Silver was not, in fact, mined here; no precious metals were found in a test shaft sunk by the Dutch East India Company. Manganese ore was once mined from the slopes above Hout Bay. The Cape of Good Hope Nature Reserve came into being in 1940 and is managed by the Western Cape Regional Services Council to preserve its animals and its unique fynbos.

Table Mountain was declared a Natural and Historical Monument in 1951. Despite this, the complexity of ownership and responsibility for the mountain (three government departments, the Cape Town City Council, the Western Cape Regional Services Council, the Cape Department of Nature Conservation, the National Botanic Gardens and private owners) has meant that no overall plan for its conservation has been accepted despite recommendations for such a plan over thirteen years ago. The areas on Table Mountain under the jurisdiction of the Council, which include the front face, the Front and Back Tables and the western slopes, are a nature reserve.

A constant problem on Table Mountain and surrounding natural areas is the wear and tear on footpaths and erosion caused by the dislodging and loosening of soil and rocks by the passage of thousands of boots, followed by water run off in winter. Although the repair and upkeep of the paths is the responsibility of the authority on whose land they lie, this work is coordinated by a standing committee with representatives from Cape Town City Council's Parks and Forest section, the Department of Nature Conservation, the Department of Environment Affairs, the Western Cape Regional Services Council and the Mountain Club of South Africa. This committee decides which paths should receive priority and it will also recommend the closure of a path that is in such poor repair that it becomes hazardous, for example the path up Blinkwater Ravine.

CONSERVATION

The concept that functioning ecosystems should be conserved and preserved is very new; in the past, only a few individuals recognised that man's effect on the environment was destructive. Only very recently has it been realised that, globally, man's very survival depends on the conservation of sufficient natural areas. All living organisms are adaptable, but at a rate which depends on the roughly constant rate of genetic mutation. Modern man's technology has imposed changes on natural systems at a rate which can far exceed the natural ability of animals, plants and insects to adapt, and often the result is extinction. The proximity of Table Mountain to a growing city for more than 300 years has resulted in great pressure on its plant and animal life. The remaining natural (more or less) areas on Table Mountain and the Peninsula are unique and must be preserved.

The greatest threats to the remaining natural areas on the Peninsula and Table Mountain are urban encroachment, squatting, invasion by alien plants (for example hakeas, acacias and pines) and animals (for example feral cats and dogs), the physical pressure of too many people walking them (which can lead to erosion and trampled vegetation) and, most importantly, too frequent fires.

Plant Invaders
The Europeans who settled the Cape introduced species of plants from different parts of the world in an attempt to correct problems which had arisen as a result of their over-exploitation of indigenous resources. Plantations of several exotic trees were established to replace depleted natural forests as sources of timber. Amongst these was the Cluster pine (*Pinus pinaster*) which, because its winged

The Port Jackson, Acacia saligna, *has become one of the most invasive pests in lowland fynbos – beautiful but destructive.*

seeds can be carried large distances by the wind, soon colonised large areas of the mountains. Enormous numbers of Australian wattles (*Acacia longifolia, Acacia cyclops* or Rooikrans, and *Acacia saligna* or Port Jackson willow) and species of *Hakea* (*Hakea sericea, Hakea gibbosa* and *Hakea suaveolens*), Australian members of the Protea family, were planted on the Cape Flats to stop the movement of dune sands which had resulted from the overgrazing and burning of their original plant cover. These Australian imports were very successful in stabilising the dunes but, within a few decades, were proliferating far beyond the area where they were first planted.

All these exotic plants enjoyed a competitive advantage over indigenous species. Whereas the mechanisms for seed dispersal were readily provided by local conditions (wind, water flow) or birds, there were in the Cape none of the predating organisms which kept their numbers in check in their natural home. Within a few decades, it was evident that these plants were out of control and were replacing the natural vegetation of large areas.

Earlier this century, some impenetrable thickets of *Hakea*

SAFETY AND RESPONSIBILITY

Some recommendations about safety are necessary as fatalities on Table Mountain are not uncommon.

✦ As regards personal safety, it is not wise to walk alone, especially on the longer and higher routes.

✦ Someone at home should know where you are going and when you expect to be back; keep to your route and use a reliable map. Beware of passing time especially in winter when daylight hours are shorter.

✦ Sensible walkers ensure that they carry warm wind- and waterproof clothing; a 'space-blanket' weighs next to nothing and can save a life.

✦ Table Mountain sandstone is hard and abrasive; comfortable shoes or boots with thick soles are a must.

✦ The high level of ultraviolet radiation in the Cape means that headgear is strongly recommended.

✦ Keep an eye on the weather. On Table Mountain and other peaks, cloud can appear within a minute as winds strengthen, particularly when the south-easter blows in summer. If you become lost in the mist or in the dark, find shelter, keep dry and warm and *don't move* until you can see where you are and where to go. *Don't panic*. There are many very steep and dangerous kloofs down Table Mountain which can be deathtraps to panicking hikers.

✦ It is always wise to carry enough liquid and some food. Given the high volume of human and canine traffic on some of the routes, I would be reluctant to drink the water.

✦ Be aware of your own level of fitness. A perfectly safe route can become a dangerous nightmare to someone who is exhausted.

Responsibility

As regards responsibility, the remaining natural areas of the Peninsula are precious and need to be protected and conserved for the future. Treat them with respect and educate others to do the same.

Do Not

✦ Pick flowers or collect mementoes; the fines which can be imposed on conviction for these offences are now high enough to be real deterrents.

✦ Write graffiti of any kind; this type of vandalism is an affront and an offence.

✦ Light a fire anywhere; or discard lit cigarette ends.

✦ Leave any litter on the mountain; take every bit of rubbish home for disposal.

✦ Take shortcuts; on steep slopes these cause erosion.

were eradicated but it is only recently that comprehensive efforts have been made by the responsible authorities to eliminate these invasive aliens from the areas of the Cape Peninsula under their control.

Dense stands of aliens can only be removed by cutting or felling, but in the case of the acacias and hakeas, insects which attack the fruits of these plants in their native Australia have been imported to help reduce their spread. After vigorous testing to ensure that it does not predate any indigenous species of plant, the *Hakea* fruit weevil (*Erytenna consputa*) has been released into *Hakea* colonies and is proving particularly successful in limiting seed production. An Australian wasp which stings the fruits of *Acacia longifolia* is proving effective here. A fungus, thought to be indigenous to South Africa, is now infecting and killing increasing numbers of hakeas in the veld.

Why go to all the trouble and expense of getting rid of these plants if they are so well adapted? The main reason is a value judgement – not controlling their numbers will lead to the loss of indigenous plants, animals and insects which are considered precious. There are two other very important and practical reasons, however. Fynbos never grows large masses of plant cover. Because of this, it does not draw large volumes of water from the soil through transpiration and, in a fire, the amount of fuel is limited. The alien species transpire far greater volumes of water than indigenous fynbos plants, a factor which reduces run off in sensitive catchment areas. Water is probably the most precious and limiting resource in South Africa today. In addition, the alien species grow more densely than the natural cover in fynbos areas; fires are fiercer and more difficult to control.

Fire sweeps down the slopes of Devil's Peak consuming everything in its path.

FIRE

At one time or another, fire has devastated much of the fynbos on the Table Mountain Range and the Cape of Good Hope Nature Reserve. Most of these fires have been caused by the carelessness of a few individuals, some by deliberate arson and some when planned burns by the authorities have run out of control. Natural fires started by lightning strikes during thunderstorms occur only rarely in the south-western Cape. In February 1990, for example, lightning started a fire on Fernwood Buttress above Newlands which burnt on the inaccessible cliff ledges for two days before being brought under control by fire-fighters.

Fire is an integral part of the ecology of the fynbos. It allows the regeneration of veld in which plants have become too old and crowded to grow and propagate successfully. The diversity of the fynbos is also reflected in the age of the veld after a fire. There is a natural succession of plant life following a fire, starting with the dominance of bulbous plants and herbs which are later supplanted by the overgrowth of the longer-lived, slower growing shrubs. The spectacular flowering of many of the bulbous plants, the Fire lilies, Watsonias, and many others, only occurs just after or within a year or two of fire. However, too frequent fires and fires in the wrong season, have an adverse effect on the diversity of the fynbos. Plants which take many years to grow and set seed can be eliminated. During the last few decades the plant life of Table Mountain has been burnt on an average every seven years which is too often for its preservation.

The Fire lily, Cyrtanthus ventricosus, *only ever blooms directly after fire. Flower heads start to appear within two weeks.*

The April fool flower, Haemanthus sanguineus, *flowers most often and plentifully after fire.*

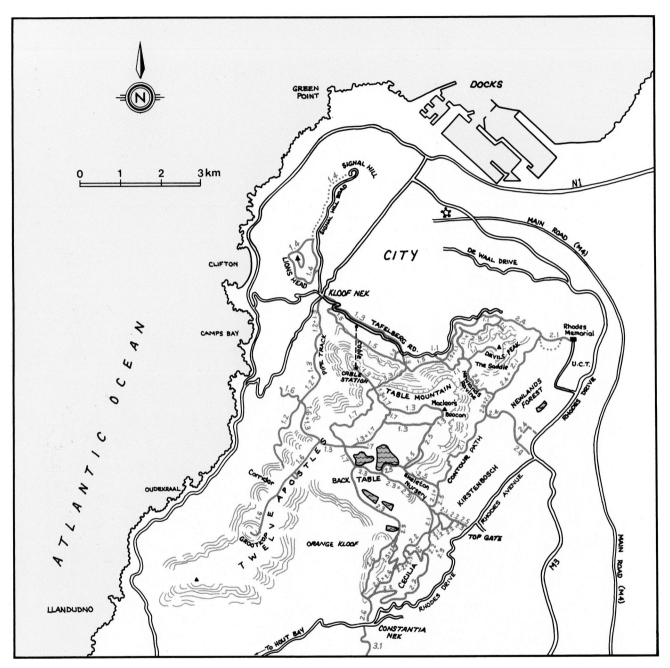

WALKS ON TABLE MOUNTAIN

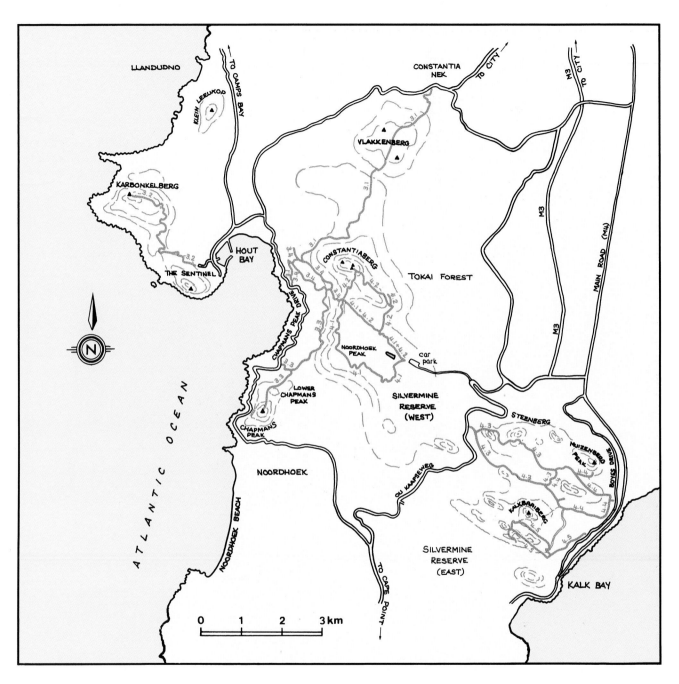

LLANDUDNO

KLEIN LEEUKOP ▲

TO CAMPS BAY

KARBONKELBERG

THE SENTINEL ▲

HOUT BAY

CONSTANTIA NEK

TO CITY

M3

TO CITY

VLAKKENBERG ▲
▲

TOKAI FOREST

MAIN ROAD (M4)

M3

CHAPMANS PEAK DRIVE

CONSTANTIABERG ▲
▲

NOORDHOEK
PEAK

car park

SILVERMINE
RESERVE
(WEST)

STEENBERG

MUIZENBERG
PEAK ▲

BOYES DRIVE

A T L A N T I C   O C E A N

N

LOWER
CHAPMANS
PEAK ▲

CHAPMANS
PEAK ▲

NOORDHOEK

NOORDHOEK BEACH

OU KAAPSEWEG

KALKBAAIBERG ▲

SILVERMINE
RESERVE
(EAST)

KALK BAY

TO CAPE POINT

0   1   2   3 km

WALKS FROM HOUT BAY AND SILVERMINE

33

CHAPTER 1

WALKS FROM KLOOF NEK

FAR LEFT: *Looking north from the top of Grootkop along the Twelve Apostles.* LEFT: Oxalis polyphylla *is one of a large number of sorrels found on the Cape Peninsula.*

In this chapter are grouped walks which are approached from Kloof Nek. The area covered by the walks comprises the front face, Front Table and west face of Table Mountain and along the Twelve Apostles, Devil's Peak, Lion's Head and Signal Hill. Because of the easy access from town, this has for generations been a popular walking area and the mountain slopes are crisscrossed with paths. Many of the minor paths on Table Mountain lead to well-known rock-climbing ascents. The major walking routes are obvious and generally maintained in good condition.

The tarred Tafelberg Road, which leads from Kloof Nek past the Lower Cable Station across the front face of Table Mountain to the north side of Devil's Peak, runs along what used to be the Contour Path on this part of the mountain. Along it are four major starting points for walks on the front face and Devil's Peak, namely Kloof Corner, Platteklip Gorge, the Saddle Path and the eastern end of the Upper Contour Path on the north side of Devil's Peak. Roughly parallel to Tafelberg Road along its whole length is the Upper Contour Path which runs east from Kloof Corner under the cliffs and intersects the Platteklip Gorge and Saddle paths before it meets Tafelberg Road on the northern slopes of Devil's Peak. The Top Contour Path branches from the Upper Contour Path just east of Silver Stream, meets the Saddle Path and continues at this level from Breakfast Rock on the Saddle and around Devil's Peak before dropping down and joining the path to Woodstock Cave from the Upper Contour Path just before this path meets Tafelberg Road.

On the Saddle itself there is a profusion of small paths. The main path over the Saddle, which leads from Breakfast Rock to the head of Newlands Ravine, is the starting point for the path up Devil's Peak. It is worth noting that there is no easy route up Table Mountain from the Saddle. The popular Ledges Route is rated a C rock climb. Newlands Ravine is a steep but safe route down the eastern side of the Saddle (*see* Chapter 2), but it is flanked by two very steep and dangerous gorges. There are paths on Devil's Peak other than those described here, but all of these require some rock-climbing skills.

On the western flank of Table Mountain, access to Kasteelspoort is gained from the Pipe Track. Kasteelspoort is an easy route up the mountain. From it a path branches south to Grootkop, and other paths lead to Maclear's Beacon and the Upper Cable Station, and also the Back Table. Platteklip Gorge is a longer, steeper route up Table Mountain than Kasteelspoort and leads directly to the Front Table from Tafelberg Road. On the top of Table Mountain there are major paths linking Kasteelspoort with Platteklip Gorge, Maclear's Beacon, and the access routes to the Back Table (*see* Chapter 2).

1.1 Devil's Peak

An ascent of Devil's Peak via the Saddle Path and a return via the Top Contour Path, Woodstock Cave and Upper Contour Path

Time: 4¼ hours.

Exertion: High.

Height climbed: 600 m.

Start: On Tafelberg Road, 4,1 km from Kloof Nek.

Route summary:
1. A fairly steep zigzag climb up the Saddle Path (35 minutes).

2. A steep climb up Devil's Peak (1 hour); and descent on the same path (30 minutes).
3. A level walk on the Top Contour Path, finally dropping to meet the path to Woodstock Cave (35 minutes).
4. A detour to Woodstock Cave (10 minutes).
5. Zigzags down the Woodstock Cave Path to meet a

level path leading left to the Upper Contour Path/Tafelberg Road junction (15 minutes).
6. A walk, gently climbing, then level, on the Upper Contour Path to meet the Saddle Path (1 hour).
7. Zigzags down the Saddle Path to start (10 minutes).

Options: A shorter walk can be made by returning

from the Saddle to the start down Saddle Path.

Links: Newlands Ravine (2.4); Contour Paths from the Upper and Top Contour Path (2.1 and 2.4).

Difficult terrain: On the Top Contour Path there is a wide, safe ledge to cross under the cliffs with a short, sheer drop below.

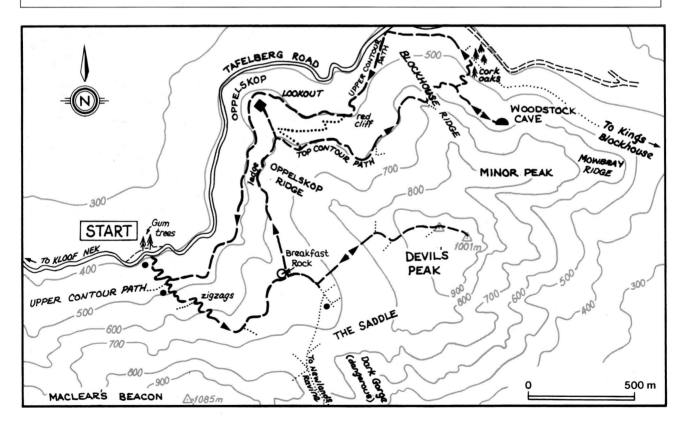

The Saddle Path starts on Tafelberg Road 2,5 km from the Lower Cable Station, across the road from some blue gum trees under which there is space to park. The start is marked with a nature reserve notice indicating what is and is not allowed on the mountain. Stone steps lead into a series of zigzags which climb straight up the slope through plant cover which shows signs of too frequent burning, a feature of this part of the mountain. After about 10-15 minutes the path crosses the Upper Contour Path and continues to zigzag up the slope. The path has been stepped and even paved with rocks in places to prevent erosion, and short stretches of rather unsightly fencing have been erected to prevent a direct path being created. After a further 8-10 minutes a path joins from the west (right). This is the link path from Silver Stream which branches off the Upper Contour Path just east of the stream to start what becomes the Top Contour Path on the Saddle. There is a good view into Platteklip Gorge from the path as it continues to zigzag more steeply through Waboom bushes and aristea plants before levelling off and heading on the contour over a small scree belt to Breakfast Rock on the Saddle; this section requires 8-10 minutes of steady walking. Some

low stone walls have been built under Breakfast Rock, which provides good shelter, especially from north-westerly winds and rain.

The Saddle Path provides some interesting comparisons. The dry, lower shale slopes support vegetation which has been burnt too often and is impoverished as a result. As one climbs, the shale gives way to Table Mountain sandstone and the plant cover changes. The rainfall on the Saddle is high and this is reflected in the richness of the fynbos both here and on the south-east slope of Devil's Peak. Ground Woodpeckers can often be seen perched on the rocks on the Saddle.

From Breakfast Rock, the best path leading to the path up Devil's Peak starts just to the north of the rock; another path leads along the stream in the same direction, but is wet in winter. The path up Devil's Peak leads straight off the former. Parallel to and to the right (east) of the path are two tracer belts; these are not recognised paths. The path leads to the highest beacon through a lovely stretch of

Above the Saddle, between Table Mountain and Devil's Peak, with Muizenberg mountain in the far distance.

fynbos, passing the slightly lower western beacon on the ridge. It takes 50-60 minutes of steady climbing on the rather badly eroded and loose path to reach the summit. The beacon is on a jumble of large rocks, and from here there are magnificent views all around, but particularly of the north face of Table Mountain, and Constantiaberg and the Muizenberg and Simon's Town mountains to the south. Devil's Peak is only 84 m lower than Maclear's Beacon, which is clearly visible. There are other paths down Devil's Peak on the eastern and northern flanks, but these are steep and not recommended. To return to Breakfast Rock, take the same path you came up. Gravity being what it is, this takes less than half the time of the ascent.

For those interested in finding the top of Newlands Ravine, the path from Breakfast Rock over the Saddle leads past the start of the path and tracer belts up Devil's Peak and shortly reaches a sign to the right pointing to New-lands Ravine (south); this path leads through a dense stand of *Protea lepidocarpodendron*, one of the 'bearded' proteas, and up a rise before it swings left to the head of Newlands Ravine. There is a confusion of small paths on the Saddle. The top of Dark Gorge is on the level of the Saddle, not up the rise, and it scarcely needs the notice which warns that this descent is dangerous. There are no walking routes up Table Mountain from the Saddle.

The Top Contour Path leaves Breakfast Rock from its north-eastern side and leads down the north-west side of the Saddle through a series of zigzags past some anti-ero-

FAR LEFT: *In December, the slopes of Table Mountain above the Saddle are carpeted with pink watsonias.* CENTRE: *The Top Contour Path leaves Breakfast Rock on the Saddle to head under the cliffs to Oppelskop.* ABOVE: *The tall dense fynbos on the Saddle below the Knife Edge is an indication of high rainfall.*

sion fences before leading around Devil's Peak on the contour. On this stretch the path is cut into a steep slope and at one point it crosses a rock ledge with a sheer but short drop. The ledge is wide, however, and not likely to cause anyone concern. What may cause discomfort if touched are the many blister bushes in this area. Some 15-20 minutes from Breakfast Rock a path drops down left (north-west) to a small nek and Oppelskop. There is a ruin of a forestry look-out post here, and the kop itself is a marvellous viewpoint. The Top Contour Path now continues on the north side of Devil's Peak. Some 10 m from the Oppelskop junction, a path leads back west towards Oppelskop in the first of a series of zigzags down to the Upper Contour Path; this is a convenient shortcut for those

running out of time. The Top Contour Path continues roughly eastward on the level. On a northern slope about 15 minutes from Oppelskop the path drops through a short section of zigzags to a junction. The right hand path leads to Woodstock Cave, which is worth a few minutes' detour; the cave is really an overhang, but is much larger than it looks from afar. The left hand path zigzags down (about ten minutes' walking time) to join a path just to the west

PROTEA GRANDICEPS

Protea grandiceps is one of the most beautiful of South Africa's proteas. A stout, rounded shrub, 1 to 1,5 m high with broad, rounded, smooth, grey-green leaves, it carries flower heads the bracts of which are a unique apricot-pink colour tipped with a white or brown beard. In nature, it is confined to some high peaks in the south-western and southern Cape. In 1854, Dr Carl

Wilhelm Ludwig Pappe, the first Colonial Botanist of the Cape and first Professor of Botany at the South African College (now the University of Cape Town), wrote, 'When 24 years ago I arrived in the Colony, *Protea coccinea* [now *grandiceps*], one of the handsomest of the proteaceous tribe, adorned the sloping sides of the Devil's Head mountain. Since that period this beautiful shrub has gradually disappeared, and seems now to have been almost annihilated.'

Originally, *P. grandiceps* was found on Table Mountain from Devil's Peak along the Front Face and along the western slopes to Corridor Buttress. Along the Twelve Apostles, it was last seen on Spring Buttress in 1942 by Miss Elsie Esterhuysen, a botanist attached to the Bolus Herbarium at the University of Cape Town. Prof W.P.U. Jackson photographed what he considered the last remaining bush on the Saddle in the early 1960s.

There is no doubt that the reason for the disappearance of this species on Table Mountain is repeated burning at short intervals. *P. grandiceps* is slow growing, flowering in nature for the first time only seven or eight years after germination of its seed. This species has not been completely eliminated from the mountain, however. In August 1989, Mr R. Buchanan recorded encountering one plant on the ledges to the east of Platteklip Gorge. In September 1990, I was lucky to come across two mature bushes in the vicinity of Devil's Peak. With adequate conservation, there is no reason why this species should not flourish where it once grew on the mountain.

of a grove of cork oaks. (This path leads east on the contour to the King's Blockhouse.) Five minutes' walking to the west brings one to a junction with the Upper Contour Path a few metres before it meets the Tafelberg Road.

Either Tafelberg Road or the Upper Contour Path can be used to return to the start of this walk. The more interesting is the Upper Contour Path, which rises gently as it rounds Devil's Peak through some dense fynbos bushes before traversing the remains of the old Plantation Path (now an

eroded gully under blue gums, once a route up Devil's Peak) and continuing to the junction with the Saddle Path. From Tafelberg Road to the Saddle Path takes 50-60 minutes of easy walking.

This walk involves some fairly strenuous climbing, but the views and the diversity of plants are rewarding. The total *walking* time is about four hours.

OPPOSITE: *High cliffs dominate the Top Contour Path.*

1.2 THE PIPE TRACK

A walk along the Pipe Track to Slangolie Ravine and back along the same path

Time: 3 hours.

Exertion: Light.

Height climbed: 150 m.

Start: Kloof Nek.

Route summary:
A virtually level walk from Kloof Nek to Slangolie Ravine (90-95 minutes) and back.

Options: A shorter walk starts in Theresa Drive in Camps Bay (1.6) For details, *see* page 64.

Link: Kasteelspoort to the Back Table (1.6).

Difficult terrain: The last part of the walk in Slangolie Ravine consists of slippery steps in disrepair, and requires care.

The Pipe Track runs more or less on the level from Kloof Nek to Slangolie Ravine on the western flank of Table Mountain and along the Twelve Apostles – a distance of about 7 km. It is an extension of the Contour Path/Tafelberg Road at the same elevation, but the aspect and views are totally different. The walk traverses the driest area covered by walks in this book and is also distinguished by the granite outcrops that are evident along the way; this is reflected in the plant life found here.

The walk starts at some stone steps which rise from the Table Mountain side of Kloof Nek just to the west of the Tafelberg Road turn-off. Parking is available a few metres along Tafelberg Road.

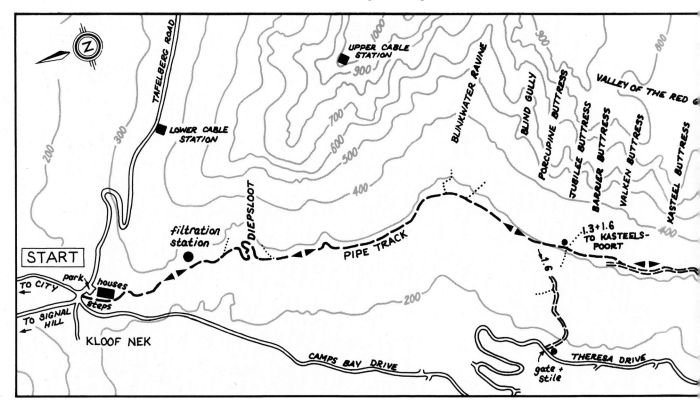

The winter-flowering daisy,
Euryops abrotanifolius, *occurs
commonly in masses along the
Pipe Track below Table Mountain and the Twelve Apostles.*

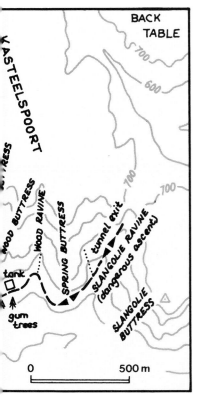

KASTEELSPOORT

BACK
TABLE

700

600

700

700

WOOD BUTTRESS

WOOD RAVINE

SPRING BUTTRESS

tunnel exit

SLANGOLIE RAVINE
(dangerous ascent)

tank

gum
trees

SLANGOLIE
BUTTRESS

0   500 m

The steps lead up next to some forestry staff houses before the path levels off under Stone pines, which shade the first kilometre or so. The pipeline, which was the original reason for the path, is soon evident where it crosses the first gully. Granite boulders are characteristic of this first part of the way. The Kloof Nek filtration plant, a rather fine-looking building, is passed on the left before the path drops steeply

LEFT: Leucospermum conocarpodendron ssp conocarpodendron *is a rare subspecies confined to granite-derived soils and is prominent along the first part of the Pipe Track.*
BELOW LEFT: *An early morning view across Camps Bay.*
BELOW: *The reason for the Pipe Track, the long pipeline which still carries water from the reservoirs on Table Mountain to the Kloof Nek filtration plant.*

into a gully called Diepsloot and emerges to continue on the level to the signposted start to Blinkwater Ravine, previously a popular way up Table Mountain but now closed to the public due to rock falls. It takes about 40-45 minutes of easy walking to reach this point.

Another 15-20 minutes on the level in open veld dotted with large bushes of Kreupelhout (the pincushion *Leucospermum conocarpodendron*) brings you to the start of the walk up Kasteelspoort, which is signposted under some blue gum trees. The pincushions are of a rare subspecies which grows naturally only on Devil's Peak and in this area, on granite clays. They differ from the other more common subspecies on the Peninsula and elsewhere in that they have hairs on the leaves which give them a characteristic silvery look.

Shortly after the Kasteelspoort turn-off the path is joined by a dirt track heading up the slope from Theresa Drive in Camps Bay (*see* page 64). The way continues along this track before it comes to an end. This point marks the exit of the Apostles Tunnel, built in 1964, through which water from the reservoirs on Table Mountain now reaches the pipeline to Kloof Nek. The rest of the Pipe Track follows the old pipeline, now defunct, which was first built to carry water from the Woodhead Tunnel. This tunnel emerges in Slangolie Ravine, the end of this route.

A short distance beyond the end of the track it becomes a path again. To the seaward side there is a dense stand of wind-clipped Spider gums (*Eucalyptuus lehmannii*), which give off a strong camphor scent on a hot, still afternoon. The path passes a small, windowless stone building – once

a surge tank and part of the original waterway. The vegetation changes character along the next stretch of the path (no longer fynbos but rather renosterbos) before it enters the aptly named Woody Ravine. From Woody Ravine the track rises on a steep slope and rounds the next bend to enter Slangolie Ravine, the end of the path. Both Woody and Slangolie ravines are surprisingly wooded, considering the drought-adapted vegetation on the neighbouring slopes: when damp, the path in Slangolie Ravine is muddy, and can be slippery. A series of steps leads finally to the steep path up to the Woodhead Tunnel exit. At this point there is the first of several signs warning that the ascent to the tunnel exit is dangerous. Since the final climb to the

The Pipe Track runs along the lower slopes of the Twelve Apostles above Camps Bay.

tunnel exit on two rickety steel ladders is barred by a padlocked gate, there is no point in attempting to reach it and you should turn around at the first sign. The rock bed in Slangolie Ravine itself is steep, loose and unstable and should on no account be climbed. Only the trees at the top seem to prevent the rock from falling.

It takes 25-30 minutes to reach Slangolie Ravine from the Kasteelspoort turn-off. The return to Kloof Nek takes the same time as the outward trip – approximately 1½ hours' walking time.

1.3 MACLEAR'S BEACON

A walk up Platteklip Gorge to Maclear's Beacon, through Echo Valley to Woodhead Reservoir, then down Kasteelspoort and back along the Pipe Track

Time: 6-7 hours.

Exertion: Very high.

Height climbed: 900 m.

Start: Kloof Nek.

Route summary:
1. A walk along Tafelberg Road from Kloof Nek to the start of the Platteklip Gorge Path (30 minutes).
2. A sustained and very steep climb up Platteklip Gorge to the Front Table (1 ¾-2 hours).
3. A level stroll to the Upper Cable Station (20 minutes there and back).
4. A stroll to Maclear's Beacon (35 minutes).
5. A largely downhill walk from Maclear's Beacon through Echo Valley to the Overseer's cottage at Woodhead Reservoir (70-80 minutes).
6. A level walk from the Overseer's cottage to the top of Kasteelspoort, then steeply down the poort to the junction with the Pipe Track (60-75 minutes).
7. A level walk back to Kloof Nek along the Pipe Track (40-45 minutes).

Options: There is a short-cut from the head of Platteklip Gorge to the top of Kasteelspoort (1.7) and a shortcut off the Front Table to Echo Valley (1.7) which excludes Maclear's Beacon. Emergency descents can be made down Platteklip Gorge or by cable car.

Links: From Maclear's Beacon via Nursery Ravine (2.3) or Skeleton Gorge (2.5); the concrete road from Woodhead Reservoir to Constantia Nek (2.3).

Difficult terrain: The path from Echo Valley to Woodhead Reservoir crosses a rock with a short, sheer drop below, but there is a fixed chain as a hand-hold; directly beyond, the path runs along a safe, concreted ledge.

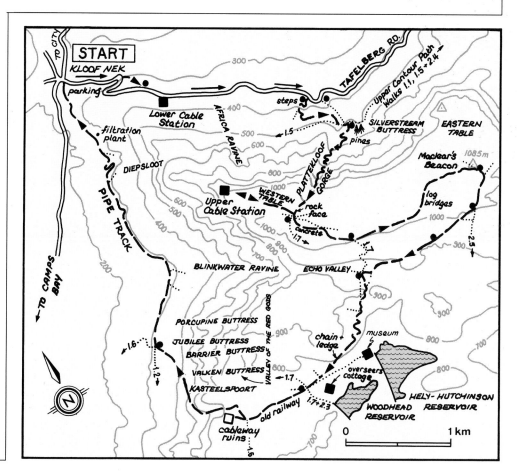

This circular route is long and in places arduous, and should be undertaken only by those who are reasonably fit. Platteklip Gorge is the only walking route up the north face of Table Mountain, and is quite demanding. Although you could descend the same way, it is well worthwhile to extend the route as described.

The walk can start anywhere on Tafelberg Road between Kloof Nek and the start of the path up Platteklip Gorge but, for reasons which will be appreciated at the end of the walk, it is best to leave your car (if you are using private transport) at the parking spot just a few metres along Tafelberg Road from Kloof Nek.

It takes 30-35 minutes to walk the 3 km from Kloof Nek along Tafelberg Road to the start of the ascent of the mountain up Platteklip Gorge. A signposted footpath – a shortcut to the Lower Cable Station – leads off left from one of the first bends on Tafelberg Road, but there is little advantage gained in taking it. Keep to the right if you take this path, otherwise it joins a gravel track across the slopes at a lower level than Tafelberg Road. From the lower cableway station, walk along Tafelberg Road until you see a high embankment built from stone and retained with wire netting.

You have a choice of two paths up Platteklip Gorge to the Upper Contour Path. The first leaves Tafelberg Road just before the embankment and is marked with a nature reserve sign: stone steps lead up the slope. Ignore a stepped path to the right which leads to one of the spotlight installations used to illuminate Table Mountain at night. The correct path leads up the shale slopes, then contours left to meet Platteklip Gorge where the Upper Contour Path crosses it. Cross the stream (here running down a series of red shale ledges) and climb a few metres up the east side, then leave the kloof on the Upper Contour Path at a point where a sign says 'Platteklip Gorge/Contour Path'.

The second path up Platteklip Gorge from Tafelberg Road to the Upper Contour Path starts at a sign indicating 'Platteklip Gorge' just beyond the stone embankment and to the left of a small dam. This path leads more steeply up the eastern side of the kloof and emerges on the Upper Contour Path just a few metres east of where it crosses the Gorge. Both routes take about 15 minutes.

About 25 m east along the Upper Contour Path, the Platteklip Gorge turns right up the mountain at a sign reading 'Contour Path/Platteklip Gorge'. The stone steps are the first of many which lead up the kloof on a long series of zigzags, becoming increasingly steep. There are

FAR LEFT: *The steep path up Platteklip Gorge.* ABOVE: *The plaque on Maclear's Beacon.*

anti-erosion fences at places to prevent a more direct route being taken. It is politic to stop occasionally to regain your breath and enjoy the view as you gain height. The higher you climb, the more the cliffs alongside the kloof close in until, near the top, the gorge is only a few metres wide. The path emerges on the Front Table flanked by two beacons of the Mountain Club of South Africa. The climb up Platteklip Gorge from the Upper Contour Path can take 1-2 hours, depending on your fitness.

At the top, a sign shows the directions of Maclear's Beacon, Platteklip Gorge and the Upper Cable Station. The Upper Cable Station is ten minutes' walk along a concrete path marked with small yellow grysbok signs; this path first climbs some rocks, then heads directly to the cable station on the level. On a fine day, it is usually thronged with visitors who have taken the far less strenuous alternative – the cableway. It is worthwhile to join them and enjoy the exceptional views north and south from this area.

The path to Maclear's Beacon rises out of the depression at the head of Platteklip Gorge and leads directly eastwards on the level. In contrast to the vegetation in Platteklip Gorge, which changes only a little as one climbs (because the upper reaches are wetter), there is an abrupt transition

to the right (west). Take the right-hand branch, which runs obliquely down a wet slope on a path stepped with logs to the corner of the fence which encloses the prohibited area surrounding the Woodhead and Hely-Hutchinson reservoirs. It takes about 15 minutes to get there. At this point another sign points the way to Blinkwater Ravine and Kasteelspoort. The path, paved with logs which can be slippery when wet, runs west along the dilapidated fence until it reaches another corner where the fence and path run south to a small stream in the bottom of Echo Valley. Here the path leaves the fence and heads west again to a sign at a crossroads where a path continues down the valley and the Kasteelspoort path splits off left. The walk along the fence to this crossroads takes 10 minutes, then follow the directions to Kasteelspoort.

The Kasteelspoort path leads up and over a rise, more or less following the fence south and drops steeply down the

on the top. The Maclear's Beacon path traverses the Front Table, which is characterised by its low restioid growth on peaty sand which is wet in winter. The shortness of the plant growth is an indication of the high winds which often blow across the exposed Front Table. After 5 minutes' walking east, a path joins from the south from Echo Valley and a sign indicates the directions to this valley, Maclear's Beacon and the cable station. Continue on the Maclear's Beacon path, which is marked with signs (white squares on little yellow footsteps) all the way from the top of Platteklip Gorge. Maclear's Beacon is visible all the time – a pyramidal cairn of small rocks on a natural, slightly elevated rocky platform. Two small log bridges cross gullies in a boggy area before the path leads up onto the small plateau on which Maclear's Beacon stands. It takes about 35 minutes to walk from the top of Platteklip Gorge to the beacon, from which there are exceptional views of False Bay and the Hottentots Holland Mountains to the east.

Ten metres to the east of the beacon itself there is a sign indicating the direction to Skeleton Gorge and Kasteelspoort. Take this path, which starts to drop fairly steeply through some rocks off the Front Table. Immediately there is a dramatic change in vegetation: these wet slopes, relatively protected from the wind, support the lush, dense, high fynbos characteristic of the Back Table. After 15-20 minutes of walking, the path branches at a sign indicating Skeleton Gorge straight ahead, Maclear's Beacon back and Blinkwater Ravine (closed to the public) and Kasteelspoort

other side with the reservoirs in view. At one point there is a fixed chain to use as a handhold as you climb around an awkward rock, and a short section where the path has been built up to form a ledge, but neither of these places poses any difficulties. The path drops down a short series of zigzags to the fence to the north of the reservoirs. At the bottom of this slope the path passes two of the largest Leucadendron trees, apart from the well-known Silver tree, I have ever seen. These are of the species *Leucadendron strobilinum*, which is endemic to the Peninsula. These particular plants, with trunks 30-40 cm in diameter, must be very ancient, untouched by fire for decades. It takes approximately 30-35 minutes from the Blinkwater Ravine and Echo Valley crossroads to reach the Overseer's cottage near Woodhead Reservoir.

A few metres to the west of the entrance to the fenced-off area there is a sign indicating Kasteelspoort to the west,

ABOVE LEFT: *A dassie suns itself in Platteklip Gorge.* CENTRE: *Moss gleams amongst the low tufts of restios which are typical of the stunted, wind-swept vegetation on the Front Table.*
ABOVE: *A pair of Table Mountain beauties,* Meneris Tulbaghia, *mating. This butterfly is the only pollinator of the Red disa.*

Constantia Nek to the south, and Maclear's Beacon back east. There are two short routes across the flats to the head of Kasteelspoort: one path leads directly there past the Mountain Club huts, but slightly to the south a raised track (originally the bed of a narrow gauge railway line) leads to the well-preserved remains of the upper end of what was once a cableway used to transport materials for the construction of Woodhead Reservoir. Both paths cross a path which leads south along the Twelve Apostles to Grootkop and north to Echo Valley and Platteklip Gorge. If you have visited the old cableway remains, take the path which drops down across the head of Kasteelspoort to join the main path down (this descends steeply on the north side of the poort). Where the path emerges from behind the cliff face of Kasteel Buttress, there is a flat rock in which the remains of a stanchion (part of the old cableway) are still fixed. From this rock, the path drops steeply on shale ledges before the slope eases and it meets the Pipe Track. It takes 60-75 minutes to walk down Kasteelspoort from the reservoirs to the Pipe Track, and another 40-45 minutes back to Kloof Nek.

The total walking time for this circuit is 6-7 hours. Plat-

Lady Anne Barnard's Ascent of Table Mountain

In 1795, British forces led by General J.H. Craig took possession of the Cape. In 1797 a civil Governor for the new Colony, Earl Macartney, arrived at the Cape accompanied by the new Secretary, Andrew Barnard, and his wife, Lady Anne. Since Earl Macartney was not married, Lady Anne became the First Lady of the Colony. On learning that '... no woman had ever been on the top of Table Mountain (N.B. this was not *literally* true one or two having been so) & being able to get no account of it from either the inhabitants of this town, all of whom wished it to be considered as next to an impossible matter to get to the top of it, as an *excuse for their own want of curiosity*, and having found the officers all willing to believe the natives for *ditto reason* Lazyness, there was some ambition as a motive for climbing as well as curiosity...'

Lady Anne one day climbed up Platteklip Gorge to the Front Table in the company of Mr John Barrow, '... two of my ship-mate officers ... my maid ... a couple of servants, & a couple of slaves with cold meat and wine ... At 8 oclock Mr Barrow and I with our followers set off – we reached the foot of the mountain on horseback & dismounted when we could ride no more – indeed nothing but a Human creature or an antilope could ascend such a path. ... we continued our progress thro a low foliage of all sorts of pretty Heaths & ever greens, the sun at last beginning to beat with much force down on our heads ... – that & fatigue obliged me frequently to sit down & as I had an umbrella with me, a few minutes allways recruited me ... about 12 oclock the sun begun to be so very hot, that I rejoyced at the turn of the mountain which I saw woud soon bring us into the shaddow, before we Reachd the great gully by wc we were to get out on the top ... once more we sett off and in three hours from the bottom of the hill reached the very tip top, of this great rock, looking down on the town ... with much conscious superiority ... we now produced our cold meat – our port – madeira and capewine, we made a splendid & Happy dinner after our fatigues, when I proposed a song to be sung in full chorus, not doubting that all the Hills around woud Join us, God save the King ...'

The party reached home again well after six o'clock that evening '... not more tired than I expected we shoud have been, & more than ever convinced that there are few things *impossible* when there is, in man or woman a decided & spirited wish of attainment.'

The Letters of Lady Anne Barnard, AA Balkema, 1973.

teklip Gorge on the exposed north face of Table Mountain can be hot. For those running out of time or energy at Maclear's Beacon it is best to return via Platteklip Gorge or even to use the cableway. Once committed to Kasteelspoort on leaving Maclear's Beacon, stick to this route; do not attempt to descend Blinkwater Ravine, because it is dangerous and closed to the public until the path has been repaired. All the paths are extremely well signposted and it is difficult to lose one's way in clear weather, but mist and cloud can come up within minutes on Table Mountain, so be wary of changes in the weather. *In an emergency*, the Overseer at Woodhead Reservoir will help.

The defile at the top of Platte-klip Gorge provides a narrow view of Cape Town far below.

1.4 Lion's Head

An ascent of Lion's Head from Kloof Nek, returning via the kramat on Signal Hill

Time: 2-2½ hours.

Exertion: Moderate.

Height climbed: 350 m.

Start: The beginning of the gravel track up Lion's Head, 600 m along the tarred road from Kloof Nek to Signal Hill.

Route summary:
1. A steady, gentle climb which completes a turn around Lion's Head, then an ascent of the ridge to the peak (1-1¼ hours).
2. A descent on the same route, but halfway down, a path to the kramat on Signal Hill is taken (50-55 minutes).
3. The path above the tarred road from the kramat back to the start (15 minutes).

Options: The walk can be extended from the kramat along the ridge of Signal Hill to the parking area overlooking Table Bay Harbour (20 minutes there and 20 minutes back to the start).

Difficult terrain: The use of the two sets of chains is optional as the main path avoids these.

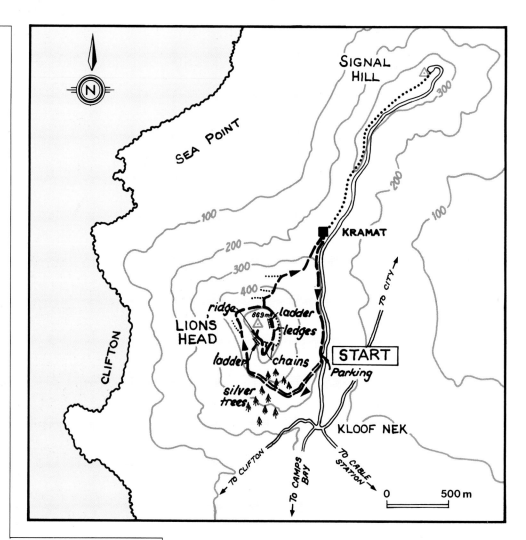

There is a fixed steel ladder up onto the first ledge. The final climb to the summit is along a rather narrow ridge on a safe path with another steel ladder.

Although Lion's Head is dwarfed by Table Mountain, its silhouette is just as well known as that of its massive neighbour's.

Lion's Head itself represents the last remains of what was a larger peak in geological antiquity; the uppermost Table Mountain sandstone rocks which rest on a resistant granite

In spring, the banks next to the path below the cliffs of Lion's Head are bright with flowers.

ABOVE: *A fixed steel ladder provides an easy way on to a ledge on the newly constructed path up Lion's Head which avoids the chains.*
RIGHT: *The path up Lion's Head provides a fine view of Clifton's beaches and yachts anchored in the clear, cold waters of the bay.*

ABOVE: *The kramat on Signal Hill is a Moslem shrine.*

evolution. Dr Andrew Smith, founder of the South African Museum, took him to see evidence of the extrusion of granite through sedimentary Malmesbury shales which is particularly clear in the rocks on the coast below the present President Hotel: this site is now a historical monument. The granite is also responsible for one of the most striking features of this peak, the grove of Silver trees (*Leucadendron argenteum*) on the south-east slopes.

Signal Hill was not always known by that name. From the time of the earliest European occupation of Cape Town it was simply called the Lion's Rump. A signalling station was first set up on the top of Lion's Head in 1673 when a flagstaff was erected and two small cannon used to alert the fort below to the arrival of vessels. An increasingly complex system of signals was used to show the number of vessels, their nationality and the direction from which they came. As shipping around the Cape increased, the workload became too much, and after the second British occupation in 1806 an intermediate signalling station was established on the Rump, which then became known as Signal Hill. This station later provided accurate times for the ships in Table Bay. Even now, the daily noon gun booms out over Cape Town and startles the pigeons who seem, over generations, never to have learnt to ignore it.

The walk starts on the gravel track which leads up Lion's Head from a parking bay on the western side of the Signal Hill road, 600 m from Kloof Nek. It leads gently up through the Silver trees, initially in a southerly direction but swinging westwards to reveal a grand vista of the Twelve Apostles and Camps Bay. The track becomes a well-worn path which continues to climb as it swings north, offering panoramic views of Clifton and Sea Point. Along the path here are some blister bushes. As the path starts to run under the cliffs on the north-west face of Lion's Head, take note of a path leading off the main path straight down the slope down some stone steps, as this is the path to take on the way back. Very shortly beyond this path the main path splits under the cliffs on the north side directly above the ridge of Signal Hill. The lower path leads to the first set of chains; these are the same chains which were fixed in 1881 by two blacksmiths to make the climb up Lion's Head easier. Unless you are keen to use this ascent, rather take the right-hand branch, a newer path which climbs up the wide ledges under the cliffs on the eastern side of Lion's Head, with the help of a fixed steel ladder at one spot. Under some ancient Stone pines the path rises to the second set of chains. Again, it is not necessary to use these

base are now almost completely weathered away. The granite rocks, which are such an evident feature of Lion's Head and its western flank, have attracted considerable scientific interest. Charles Darwin visited the Cape in 1836 on the voyage in the Beagle which was to provide the stimulus which led to his formulation of the theory of

THE SILVER TREE

Although not by any means, as many authors claim, the largest of South Africa's species of Proteaceae (that distinction belongs to *Faurea macnaughtonii*, a forest tree), the Silver tree (*Leucadendron argenteum*) can grow to an impressive size. It was one of the first plants to be collected by early visitors to the Cape and specimens were sent back to Europe as curiosities. This species grows in soils derived from weathered granite. Once far more plentiful on the northern and eastern slopes of Table Mountain, the grove on Lion's Head is the largest remaining natural population.

The silvery sheen on the leaves of the Silver tree is caused by their dense covering of light-reflecting hairs. In dry weather these hairs lie flat on the surface to prevent moisture loss, and in this condition the leaves are particularly shiny. Individual plants are male or female. Female plants produce silver cones which eventually release nut-like seeds with natural parachutes, enabling winds to carry them some distance from the tree.

to get to the top, as a clear path leads south at the level of the bottom chain to emerge on the south end of a small rocky ridge up which the path swings right through the rocks. At the end of a short level section, the path meets the way up from the second set of chains at the start of the final pull to the beacon. The path up the ridge is safe, even though the ridge falls away steeply on both sides. A second fixed steel ladder helps you up one tricky rock. From the top, there is a magnificent all-round view of Table Mountain and the Twelve Apostles, Cape Town, Table Bay, the distant mountains and the western seaboard including Robben Island and Dassen Island, 60 km away. It takes from 1-1¼ hours to climb Lion's Head.

From the summit, return the same way, or via the chains; it should take about thirty minutes to reach the place on the north side under the cliffs overlooking Signal Hill where the path meets the path from the first set of chains. A few minutes later you will see the path which leads off the main path down the slope towards Sea Point. Take this path, which very shortly meets a path running along the

contour; turn right (north). After another five minutes this path meets another lower path; turn right again. This path meets yet another lower path after eight minutes; turn right again, and follow the rather eroded path down the slope to the kramat. Notice the old cannon above and slightly to the right of the parking area that is soon reached.

The kramat is a sacred Moslem shrine, the burial place of Tuan Muhamed Hassan Gaibe Sha, who was a spiritual leader of the Malay community. It is one of a holy circle of shrines which extends as far as Faure, within which the Malay community believes it is protected from natural disasters. If you wish to enter the kramat, observe the courtesies requested and due to this part of the Cape's culture and remove your shoes.

If you wish, you can continue to the end of Signal Hill along the path which runs along the ridge to the parking area; this takes about 20 minutes there and the same back to the kramat. From here, the walk on the path above and parallel to the tarred road back to the start is an easy 15-minute stroll.

1.5 UPPER CONTOUR PATH

A walk along the Upper Contour Path from Kloof Corner to its junction with Tafelberg Road on the north slope of Devil's Peak

Time: 2 hours one way.

Exertion: Light; there is a short zigzag climb at the start, but thereafter the path is essentially on the level.

Height climbed: 200 m.

Start: On Tafelberg Road, 850 m from Kloof Nek alongside the turn-off to the filtration plant.

Route summary:
1. A fairly steep zigzag climb from Tafelberg Road to the ruined lookout on Kloof Corner (20 minutes).
2. A level walk to Platteklip Stream (30 minutes).
3. A gentle descent to the junction with the Saddle Path (25 minutes).
4. A level walk around Devil's Peak, finally dropping gently to meet Tafelberg Road (45 minutes).

5. A level walk back on Tafelberg Road to the start (1½-2 hours).

Options: From the Upper Contour Path numerous paths leading down to Tafelberg Road provide shortcuts. It is a 20-minute level walk from the eastern end of the Upper Contour Path to the King's Blockhouse above Rhodes Memorial.

Links: Platteklip Gorge and the Front Table (1.3); the Saddle, Devil's Peak (1.1) and Newlands Ravine (2.4); Top Contour Path (1.1); Contour Path (2.1 and 2.4).

Difficult terrain: None; the ledge at Silver Stream is wide, but can be slippery when wet.

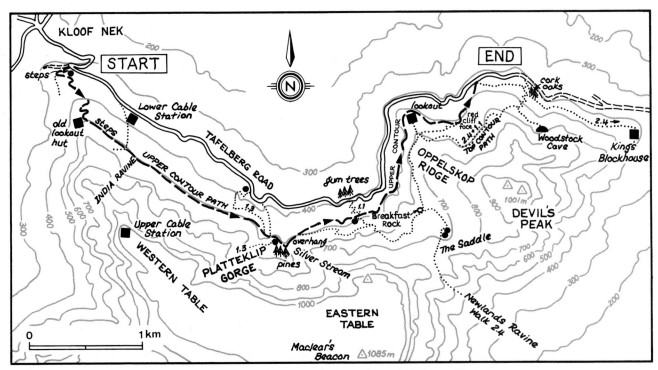

OPPOSITE: *As it crosses Silver Stream, the Upper Contour Path passes under an overhang which frames Lion's Head.*

Alongside the Upper Contour Path near Kloof Corner, the rock faces are the habitat for white daisies (above) and in seepage areas, sundews, spiloxenes and moss (top).

The Upper Contour Path on the north face of Table Mountain serves the same function as the Contour Path on the east by providing access to the routes up the front face of the mountain. (On this side of the mountain all of them, except Platteklip Gorge, are rock-climbing routes.) At the start the path runs just under impressive sandstone cliffs, but after crossing Silver Stream the path drops gently, crosses the Saddle Path and rounds Devil's Peak at a slightly lower elevation before dropping down to meet Tafelberg Road just before this comes to an end. Tafelberg Road starts at Kloof Nek. From the entrance to the Kloof Nek filtration plant it virtually runs parallel to the Upper Contour Path right across the face of Table Moun-

tain but at a lower elevation. Tafelberg Road was built over the old Contour Path.

Tafelberg Road leaves Kloof Nek and climbs to the level of the old Contour Path through a zigzag. As the road emerges from the second hairpin bend, the road to the Kloof Nek filtration plant leads off to the right. Immediately to the left of this is a nature reserve sign and stone steps leading up the slope. These are the start of the walk.

The path climbs the slope in a series of zigzags, in places stepped with logs and in others with stone, at first on granite and then on shale untill the sandstone cliffs are reached at the ruined lookout hut on Kloof Corner. The path passes under the telephone line to the Upper Cable Station. The climb takes about 20 minutes. From here there are fine views of Lion's Head, Signal Hill and Camps Bay.

The gentle, and major, part of this walk starts here as the path leads east on the contour past a seepage area which is a miniature garden in spring with Sundews (*Drosera* spp), Yellow spiloxenes and other plants flowering in the moss. A fixed chain marks the start of the C-grade rock climb, Kloof Corner. The path climbs several stone steps and then runs directly under the cliffs. Shortly there is a signposted path down to the Lower Cable Station, but the Contour Path crosses the streams in Africa and Union ravines and another stream before rounding Platteklip Buttress on the west side of Platteklip Gorge. Before the path meets the stream in the gorge, the first of the paths from Tafelberg Road up Platteklip Gorge joins it. It takes about 30 minutes to walk from the lookout hut on Kloof Corner to the Platteklip Stream, which flows down some red shale ledges at the crossing.

On the other side of Platteklip Stream the path climbs some stone steps and emerges from the kloof a few metres higher. There it meets the second path from Tafelberg Road up the gorge (on its western side) and crosses a subsidiary stream just before a sign indicating the path up Platteklip Gorge. The Upper Contour Path continues on the level around a bluff and past four old Stone pines to Silver Stream, which drops over a small waterfall in a wooded kloof. Just beyond the stream the path passes under an overhang on a wide ledge. Shortly after, the path divides. The upper path maintains its elevation and is a link to the Saddle Path, meeting this just before it heads towards Breakfast Rock on the Saddle; it is essentially the beginning of the Top Contour Path. Take the lower branch, which is the Upper Contour Path – it starts to drop gently, crossing another small stream before crossing the Saddle Path. There

At Kloof Corner, a mass of spring flowers covers the dry shale slopes below the season's first 'table cloth'.

is a sign at the crossroads indicating 'Contour Path' (the Upper Contour Path) and the Saddle. The Saddle Path provides a shortcut down to Tafelberg Road. The walk from Platteklip Stream to the Saddle Path takes 25 minutes.

The Upper Contour Path continues into a small plantation of blue gums which marks the course of an abandoned path up to the Saddle (the Plantation Path) and the beginning of its traverse of Devil's Peak. The western slopes of Devil's Peak are covered with Kreupelhout (*Leucospermum conocarpodendron*) and *Erica baccans*, which provide a colourful sight in spring. As the path turns onto the north slopes next to the sandstone cliffs under Oppelskop, however, the vegetation changes as this is a dry area. These slopes are rather bare and unattractive as the indigenous vegetation has not re-established completely. The Upper Contour Path meets a path which zigzags down the slope

from the abandoned lookout on Oppelskop itself, and passes the remains of a telephone line to it. The path drops steadily, now clearly on shale-derived soil, over two streams and past a dramatic damp red rock overhang festooned with Arum lilies and ferns shortly before it drops down to Tafelberg Road, which comes to an end just east of this point. The walk from the Saddle Path round Devil's Peak takes about 45 minutes.

Just before the Upper Contour Path meets Tafelberg Road, a path leads off to the right on the contour to the King's Blockhouse (2.4), a walk of 20 minutes. Off this is a path which climbs steeply and branches left to Woodstock Cave and right to become the Top Contour Path (1.1).

The complete traverse of the front face of Table Mountain and Devil's Peak takes only two hours and provides a wonderful panorama of Cape Town and the mountain itself from a variety of aspects. It takes somewhat less to walk along Tafelberg Road to the start if transport is not waiting at the end.

1.6 GROOTKOP

An ascent of Grootkop by way of Kasteelspoort and the path along the Twelve Apostles, returning the same way

Time: 6-7 hours from Kloof Nek; 5 hours from Theresa Drive, Camps Bay.

Exertion: Very high.

Height climbed: 900 m from Kloof Nek; 950 m from Theresa Drive.

Start: The stone steps leading up past the forestry staff houses on the Table Mountain side of Kloof Nek, a few metres west of the start of Tafelberg Road; or the track leading up the slope off Theresa Drive in upper Camps Bay.

Route summary:
1. A level walk from Kloof Nek along the Pipe Track to the start of the Kasteelspoort Path (45-55 minutes); or a moderate climb up the track from Theresa Drive in Camps Bay to the junction of the Kasteelspoort Path and the Pipe Track (15 minutes).
2. A steep climb up Kasteelspoort (55-60 minutes).

3. A traverse with moderate rises and falls from the top of Kasteelspoort to the foot of Grootkop (1 hour).
4. An ascent of Grootkop, in places steep and overgrown (35 minutes).
5. A descent from Grootkop Peak (20 minutes).
6. A return traverse from Grootkop to Kasteelspoort (50 minutes).
7. A steep climb down Kasteelspoort to the Pipe Track (45-50 minutes).
8. A level walk back along the Pipe Track to Kloof

Nek (45-55 minutes); or an easy stroll down the track to Theresa Drive (10 minutes).

Links: Echo Valley (1.7), Maclear's Beacon (1.3), Nursery Ravine and Skeleton Gorge (2.5), and the Bridle Path (2.3), all via Woodhead Reservoir.

Difficult terrain: The path up Grootkop itself is overgrown.

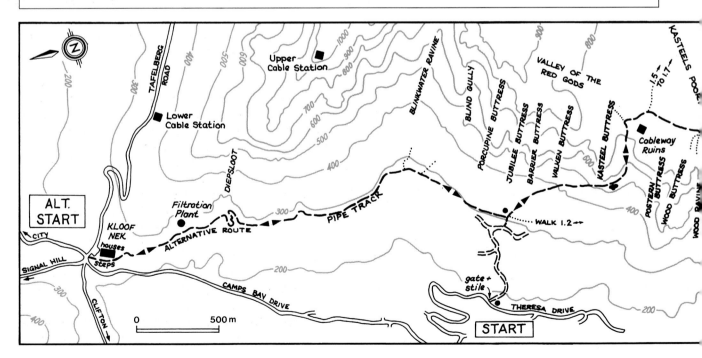

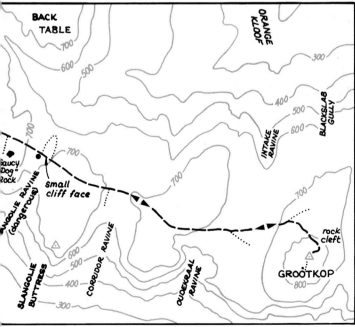

The Saucy Dog, a uniquely-shaped rock, is a landmark on the path to Grootkop, seen here in the distance.

Grootkop is one of my favourite places on Table Mountain. It stands apart from the Table Mountain massif itself, and because it is substantially higher than the top of the Twelve Apostles, the peak provides inspiring views all round. It is also frequented less than the more popular routes, so you can experience a sense of peace and isolation in magnificent surroundings here.

The start of the Kasteelspoort Path can be reached from Kloof Nek along the Pipe Track (1.2), a level walk of 45-55 minutes. Because the route from here to the top of Grootkop is fairly long and strenuous, an alternative start to the walk is given which cuts about 30 minutes off the time taken to reach the Kasteelspoort Path from Kloof Nek (a saving of an hour in all).

Drive down Camps Bay Drive from Kloof Nek. Turn left into Fiskaal Road, which swings first left then right up the slope; turn left into Francolin Road and right into Theresa

Drive. The only turn left off Theresa Drive leads straight up to a gate at the start of a forestry track up the slope. Park in Theresa Drive, but in such a way that you do not block the entrance to the forestry track or any private entrances. Walk through the stile next to the gate up the concrete strip road to a T-junction, passing a gravel road on the left. At the junction turn right. After a few metres, climb the stone steps which lead up left off the road to the blue gum trees along the Pipe Track opposite the signposted start to the path up Kasteelspoort. The walk up to the Pipe Track takes 15 minutes.

On the left-hand side of the Kasteelspoort Path there is a small plaque – recently fixed to the face of a rock – announcing that the restoration of the path is to be undertaken with funding from the South African Nature Foundation and the public. This is a worthwhile project, since Kasteelspoort is probably the most used route up Table Mountain. The path rises gently at first as it heads towards Kasteel Buttress, but more steeply as it swings south up a series of red shale ledges (all easy to negotiate) directly under the grey sandstone cliffs. Eventually it reaches a flat rocky platform on the slopes of the poort which, judging by the increasing amount of graffiti and rubbish left lying around, is a popular stopping place, especially for uncivilised people whose idea of immortality is to paint their names, and worse, on rocks. Still firmly fixed in the rock is a piece of steel rod, all that remains of one of the supports for the aerial cableway which ran up the poort to carry building materials during the construction of Woodhead Reservoir. From this rock, the path climbs steeply up the left side of the poort on a long series of rocky steps, opposite the imposing bulk of Postern Buttress. This part of the path is badly worn and certainly in need of upgrading, though never difficult to negotiate.

Before the path reaches the top of the kloof, a path branches off to the right to cross the stream and climb up the opposite slope. A little higher up, a second path does the same. Take either of the paths, which join up to reach a crossroads. The path to Grootkop leads straight on southwards. To the left is a raised track which is all that remains of a small railway which was used to carry building supplies from the head of the cableway described above. It is well worth the time to walk a few metres to the right to see the remains of the Upper Cable Station, built solidly of beautifully dressed stone like the wall of the reservoir itself. Amazingly, a piece of original timber still remains bolted to the structure. From the strategically placed platform, there is a dizzying view directly down Kasteelspoort to the sea. The rocks beyond the platform are favoured by Ground Woodpeckers, whose unmistakable call often accompanies the climb up the poort.

It takes 55-60 minutes to climb up Kasteelspoort.

The Grootkop Path heads straight towards the peak from the top of Kasteelspoort. It is immediately obvious that this is a less used route. Level at first, the path then drops gently through a vlei area to the top of Woody Ravine, where there is a sign indicating the route down this ravine off the Grootkop Path. The Grootkop Path itself continues south up a slight rise to Spring Buttress. To the right of the path there is a curiously shaped rock, supposed to look like a begging dog. The path drops down into the nek at the head of Slangolie Ravine where there is a signpost warning that

FAR LEFT: *Postern buttress looms over the steep path up Kasteelspoort.* CENTRE: *The remains of the old cable station at the head of Kasteelspoort where building supplies for the reservoirs were unloaded onto the narrow guage railway.* BELOW: *The platform provides a dizzying view down the poort to Bakoven.*

TOP: Bulbine asphodeloides, *a small member of the Lily family.*
ABOVE: Chasmanthe floribunda *seen in mid-winter along the lower stretch of the path up Kasteelspoort.*

the path leading off to the right is a 'Dangerous descent'; under no circumstances attempt it. From the nek, the path goes up a small rock face. This is not exposed and presents no great problem, but an alternative minor path which avoids it leads off left at the bottom of the nek for about 50 m, turns right up through some rocks and swings right again to join the main path above the face. Once across Slangolie Buttress, the path drops to the top of Corridor Ravine and climbs over Corridor Buttress to reach a flat area in front of Grootkop. The traverse from the top of Kasteelspoort to the foot of Grootkop takes 60 minutes.

Below Grootkop, the path divides: take the left-hand branch. This crosses a stream before climbing up onto the eastern slopes of Grootkop. From this point the path is very overgrown, which makes walking strenuous. However, the path is not difficult to follow, being marked with stone cairns along the way. The path twists and turns as it climbs up through the rocks and thick growth heading in a general south-westerly direction to reach the foot of a small gully on the higher south-east slopes. It runs straight up the gully and swings right out of it through a field of ericas before swinging left on the final pull to the beacon.

Although the ascent of Grootkop is a short distance, it takes 35 minutes of strenuous climbing to reach the top. This effort is richly rewarded – Grootkop is the highest peak in this part of the Table Mountain massif and, because it is isolated, provides a spectacular 360-degree panorama. Probably nowhere else on the Peninsula can you get such a comprehensive all-round view. It is exhilarating to sit next to the beacon and look out past the Twelve Apostles, the Upper Cable Station on Table Mountain, Lion's Head and Table Bay to the West Coast disappearing into the distance. From here, most of Orange Kloof is visible in front of the reservoirs which lie below the Front Table. The rest of the Peninsula is laid out to the south.

It takes only 20 minutes to descend Grootkop to reach the flats on its northern side, where the path leads back across the Twelve Apostles to Kasteelspoort. The climb down the rock face just above the nek at the top of Slangolie Ravine is trickier than the climb up; the alternative path is easily taken, starting to the right just above the face along the top of these rocks to an obvious place to drop down and swing left below the rocks to join the main path at the nek. The top of Kasteelspoort is reached 50 minutes after leaving the foot of Grootkop, and the climb down Kasteelspoort takes 45-50 minutes. Ten minutes' walking down the forestry track gets you back to Theresa Drive.

1.7 WOODHEAD RESERVOIR

A circular route linking the Front Table with the Woodhead and Hely-Hutchinson reservoirs and Waterworks Museum

Time: 3 hours for the circuit only. Add extra time for any ascent and descent of Table Mountain (*see* the relevant descriptions) and for a visit to the reservoir wall and the Waterworks Museum.

Exertion: Medium to high for the circuit only; high to very high if an ascent is included.

Height climbed: 450 m, excluding any ascent.

Start: This circular route can be approached from the Upper Cable Station; Platteklip Gorge (1.3); Kasteelspoort (1.6); the Bridle Path (2.3); Nursery Ravine (2.3); or Skeleton Gorge (2.5).

Route summary (from top of Platteklip Gorge)
1. A steep climb down into Echo Valley (35 minutes).
2. A moderate climb into Ark Valley and down into the Valley of Isolation (30 minutes).
3. A short, climb out of the Valley of Isolation and down to the Overseer's cottage (30 minutes).
4. A walk to the Waterworks Museum (15 minutes there and back).
5. A fairly steep zigzag climb from the reservoirs over the ridge into Echo Valley (45 minutes).
6. A steep climb up to the Front Table, then a stroll to the top of Platteklip Gorge (25 minutes).

Links: This circuit links all the walking routes up Table Mountain, as well as the cableway.

Difficult terrain: The descent from the top of Platteklip Gorge into Echo Valley involves two sections of scrambling down steep rocks.

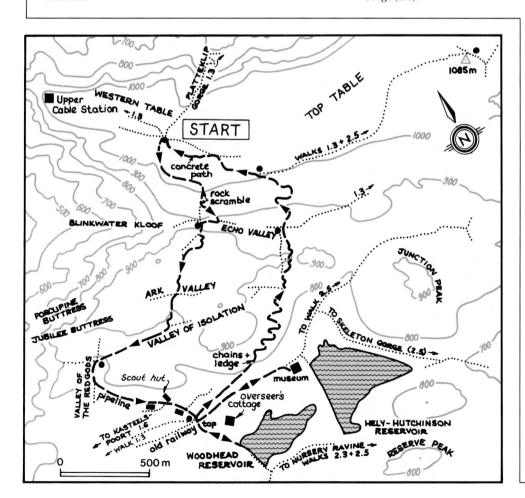

The views from the Front Table have thrilled millions of visitors; here the Twelve Apostles stretch southwards.

This circuit – which crosses Echo Valley first at its western end, then further east on the return – is an attractive walk in itself. In addition, it includes the two main routes linking the Front Table with Woodhead Reservoir: these are not described elsewhere and may be used to shorten, extend or link other walks. The circuit may be approached from any of the ascents of Table Mountain described elsewhere, and left by any of the descents. Alternatively the cableway provides an easy (although in holiday season crowded and time-consuming) way to the route. It is imperative to add sufficient time for the ascent and descent by whatever route and to take into account the extra exertion required by any of the walking ascents. The circuit is described here as starting at the top of Platteklip Gorge; if the cableway is used, it is a ten-minute stroll to the twin beacons which mark the top of Platteklip Gorge. The older beacon was erected in 1892 by the newly-formed Mountain

Club of South Africa and was a signpost; the newer beacon on the western side of the gorge commemorates the 50th anniversary of the club's founding. There is also a metal signpost with directions to Maclear's Beacon and Platteklip Gorge but no direction to Echo Valley. The path to Echo Valley is the fourth arm (leading south-west) of the crossroads at the top of Platteklip Gorge. Do not be confused by the tangle of paths leading onto the Eastern Table – the Echo Valley path lies to the west of the broad concrete path to Maclear's Beacon.

The path initially drops down the top of a steep kloof, then swings left (east) along the steep slope above Echo Valley. As it turns the first corner, there is a distant view of Bakoven between the rocky sides of the kloof. At first the path runs more or less on the contour, then starts to drop steeply where it branches, the left branch rejoining shortly. The path drops down a short, almost vertical rock face

The Hely-Hutchinson (left) and Woodhead Reservoirs lie below the ridge above Echo valley to the north.

which requires a bit of scrambling but is not at all difficult or exposed. A little further down there is another scramble, the steepest part of which can be avoided by crawling to the right under a small, low rock overhang. (Ignore paths from the left and right down this steep section.) The path drops down steeply to join the path along the bottom of Echo Valley: turn right to the signpost. Echo Valley is aptly named, as a yodel or two of satisfaction at negotiating the steep bits will demonstrate. The walk here from the top of Platteklip Gorge takes 35 minutes.

The signpost is at a crossroads; ahead is the path down Blinkwater Ravine (closed to the public), and to the right a path leads straight back up the slope – originally it was probably a tracer for a firebreak. Take the path left, which leads up the opposite slope. This shortly branches. Take the left branch (the right branch leads to the head of the kloof between Jubilee and Porcupine buttresses) which leads over the rise to a crossroads in a shallow valley, Ark Valley. Ignore the paths to right and left and climb the opposite slope. From the top of the ridge, the path drops steeply on stone steps into the Valley of Isolation. Down this slope, the path passes the turn-off to a cave on the right of the path, then leads along a damp cliff face below which the beginnings of a forest can be seen, with small Yellowwoods prominent. The Valley of Isolation is a small, well-watered enclosed valley. In the sandy bottom on the left of the path, part of the valley floor has subsided. The Valley of Isolation is reached 30 minutes after leaving Echo Valley.

From the valley bottom, where a faint path joins from the left, the path heads in a westerly direction up the slope, passing several small paths to viewpoints on the left, and drops to a crossroads, with the nek between Barrier and Valken buttresses in view ahead. At the crossroads there is a signpost showing the directions of Kasteelspoort (left)

Constantiaberg and Hout Bay form the backdrop for restios and moss on the path near Ark Valley.

In the Waterworks Museum, pride of place is given to this narrow-guage railway engine. This is a mecca for many steam-engine enthusiasts from all over the world.

and Platteklip Gorge. The path straight ahead leads over the nek to Barrier Buttress and the one to the right up the slope back into the western end of Ark Valley. The left-hand path to Kasteelspoort follows an old pipeline round the rocks left onto the slope above the Mountain Club hut and joins a broad path to this hut just to the east of it. Turn left along this path, past the Scout hut on the left and a building on the right, to the entrance to the Overseer's cottage. It is a 30-minute walk to this point from the Valley of Isolation.

It is well worth a seven-minute walk along the concrete road past the Overseer's cottage to the Waterworks Museum. This is housed in an unpretentious building near the wall of Hely-Hutchinson Reservoir. The museum contains memorabilia of the construction of the Woodhead and Hely-Hutchinson reservoirs. Pride of place is given to the small narrow-gauge railway engine which was used to haul materials from the head of the cableway up Kasteelspoort (1.6) along a raised track to the construction site. Outside the museum a part of the haulage gear from the cableway and a small railway crane used for loading and off-loading can be seen. The key for the museum should be requested from the Overseer. Another short detour can be made to the wall of Woodhead Reservoir; a path runs along the top of the wall. Let into the top course of the beautifully dressed Table Mountain sandstone of which the wall is constructed, is a granite block commemorating its completion in 1892.

The return route starts at the fenced corner at the head of the concrete road to the museum and just below the Overseer's cottage. The path runs next to the fence, passing some stone steps on the left – the start of a path straight up the slope. Further along, the path climbs up amongst some old *Leucadendron strobilinum* bushes to above a rock overhang to the right. The path crosses the overhang on a built-up concrete ledge leading to a rock with a fixed chain to help you up if it is slippery, as there is a sheer fall below. From this point, the path zigzags, climbing on stone steps up to the top of the ridge, more or less following the line of the fence. Over the top of the ridge a minor path leads off left to the junction of paths from the Valley of Isolation and Ark Valley. Ignore this and follow the path down, at first next to the fence, into Echo Valley. At the bottom there is a signpost with directions to Maclear's Beacon to the right, Kasteelspoort in the direction from which you came and left to Blinkwater Ravine. No sign points to the path you should take, which is straight ahead, crossing a

Ixia odorata *grows along the path on the shaded, steep, rocky slopes above the Overseer's Cottage at the Woodhead Reservoir.*

log bridge before it climbs the slope. The path swings to the right, avoiding a direct path up the slope, which is barred by an anti-erosion fence. It is a steep climb out of Echo Valley back to the level of the Front Table on a very good paved and stepped path which finally meets the path from the top of Platteklip Gorge to Maclear's Beacon at a signpost. It takes 65-70 minutes to walk from the Overseer's cottage at Woodhead Reservoir back to the Front Table via this route. Another 5 minutes brings you to Platteklip.

The reverse of this return route is a shorter (50-55 minutes), more direct and easier route to the reservoirs from the Front Table than the route via Ark Valley and the Valley of Isolation. Both routes traverse rich areas of wet fynbos characteristic of the high south-facing slopes, which receive high rainfall in winter and appreciable moisture from south-easter cloud in summer.

Cloud can come up very rapidly on top of Table Mountain, therefore read the weather, and know where you are and where you are going. Do not attempt an ascent or descent of Table Mountain by any route not detailed in the summary on page 47, or by any unknown route.

The Overseer at Woodhead Reservoir will provide help *in an emergency*, as will staff at the Upper Cable Station.

CHAPTER 2

TABLE MOUNTAIN'S EASTERN FACE

FAR LEFT: *The forested slopes, here dominated by Fernwood buttress, are characteristic of Table Mountain's eastern face.* LEFT: Gladiolus hyalinus, *the Small brown afrikaner, flowers in January.*

This chapter comprises six walks on the eastern side of Table Mountain and the Back Table, together with links to the routes described in Chapter 1. Unlike all the walks in Chapter 1, these are not served by a common starting point, but are linked by the Contour Path which runs from the end of Tafelberg Road on Devil's Peak (in the north) to Constantia Nek (in the south). There are five main approaches to the Contour Path in this area (starting in the north): from Rhodes Memorial, Newlands Forest, Kirstenbosch, Cecilia Forest and Constantia Nek. From the Contour Path, there is a steep but safe route up Newlands Ravine to the Saddle between Table Mountain and Devil's Peak, but from the Saddle there is no easy route up Table Mountain. The two easy but steep routes from the Contour Path up the mountain to the Back Table are Nursery Ravine and Skeleton Gorge above Kirstenbosch. There are routes up the many other gorges on this side of Table Mountain, but all involve rock climbing and should not be attempted by anyone without the necessary skills, equipment and guidance, as some of these are particularly steep and dangerous. The easiest route of all up Table Mountain is the Bridle Path from Constantia Nek through Cecilia Forest onto the Back Table. This road provides access to the reservoirs for staff maintenance; private vehicles are not allowed entry. North of Cecilia Forest paths lead from the Contour Path to the patches of natural forest in Cecilia Ravine and a small kloof north of this.

With private transport and pre-planning it is possible to combine any of the routes up Table Mountain in this chapter with descents described in Chapter 1, or vice versa, by leaving a car at the finish. The major path junctions on top of Table Mountain are at the head of Platteklip Gorge and at Maclear's Beacon, Woodhead Reservoir and the tops of Nursery Ravine and Skeleton Gorge.

This is the wet side of the mountain and substantial areas are still under more or less natural forest. Plantations of alien trees, mainly pines, were established in the Newlands and Cecilia forest areas long ago. The Cape Town City Council and the National Botanic Gardens have done a magnificent job in clearing pine infestations on the often difficult terrain under their jurisdiction, so it is incongruous that the above-mentioned two plantations are still being maintained by the Council and the Department of Environment Affairs respectively. An even greater ecological hazard is the infestation of wattles, blue gums, pines and acacias on the Groote Schuur Estate above Rhodes Memorial.

The major natural feature of the Back Table is Orange Kloof. This kloof, which splits the Back Table, starts as Disa Kloof at the wall of Woodhead Reservoir and covers a large area at the head of the Hout Bay Valley. It is off limits to the public because it is maintained as a natural area.

2.1 Contour Path

A walk along the Contour Path from Rhodes Memorial to Kirstenbosch

Time: 2¾-3 hours.

Exertion: Moderate.

Height climbed: 350 m.

Start: The parking area at Rhodes Memorial.

Route summary:
1. A steep climb from Rhodes Memorial to the Contour Path (25-30 minutes).
2. A level walk, at first on Groote Schuur Estate, then in natural forest to the turn-off to Lübbert's Gift above Kirstenbosch (1 hour).
3. A steep zigzag climb above a scree belt and down again to the contour and on to the stream in Skeleton Gorge (45 minutes).
4. A continuation of the walk on the contour, now clear of the forest, over Nursery Ravine to the junction with the Cecilia Ravine Path from Kirstenbosch (25 minutes).
5. A walk down past the reservoir through Kirstenbosch to the top gate (10 minutes).

Options: The walk can be shortened by taking any of the paths down the mountain to Newlands Forest or Kirstenbosch, or extended to Constantia Nek through Cecilia Forest.

Links: The Contour Path is the access to Newlands Ravine (2,4), Skeleton Gorge (2,5) and Nursery Ravine (2,3) above Kirstenbosch, and Cecilia Ravine (2,2).

Difficult terrain: None.

The Contour Path runs more or less on the level along the eastern side of Devil's Peak and Table Mountain, at the same elevation as Tafelberg Road on the north face. The eastern slopes of Table Mountain receive more rain than the open, dry northern slopes, and large areas are still naturally forested. Because most of the route is shaded, it is an ideal walk in hot weather.

The route starts at Rhodes Memorial. At the top of the parking area an obvious path, stepped with logs, leads up the slope. This shortly meets a gravel road. From here there are two ways up to the stile and turnstile on the Contour Path just below the King's Blockhouse where the path crosses the northern boundary of the Groote Schuur Estate (marked by a sign). The first leads straight up the slope to

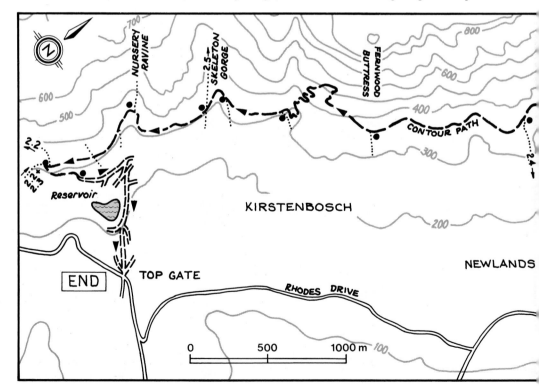

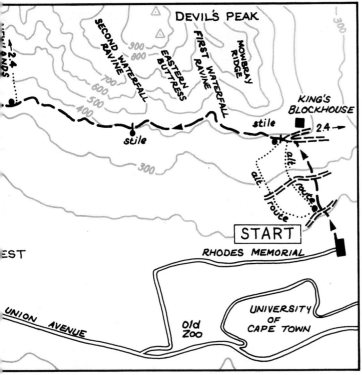

ABOVE: *The essence of the contour path – moss, rocks and trees near Newlands Ravine.*

LEFT: *A species of* Homeria *or Tulp.*

a gravel road that comes to the stile, a continuation of the path from the parking lot. The second is signposted 'Contour Path' a few metres left along the gravel road; this path follows a gentler slope in a south-westerly direction up through the Stone pines, then swings north-west through wattle trees, crossing another gravel road on the way. It takes 25-30 minutes to reach the Contour Path.

From the stile, take the higher of the two paths facing you; this is the Contour Path. It is a 15-minute walk to the southern boundary of Groote Schuur Estate, similarly marked with sign, stile and turnstile. This is the least attractive section of the route amongst the uncontrolled

LEFT: *A view of Kirstenbosch and the reservoir from the Contour Path.* TOP RIGHT: *The southern part of the Contour Path above the Kirstenbosch reservoir emerges from the forest into fynbos with Castle Rock looming above.* ABOVE: *The Contour Path crosses several scree belts – these rocks provide a glimpse of the cliffs above.*

alien pines, blue gums and wattle trees that infest an area which was once a grove of beautiful Silver Trees. The path crosses a stream from First Waterfall Ravine between Devil's Peak and Mowbray Ridge and a subsidiary stream in Second Waterfall Ravine.

South of the Groote Schuur Estate boundary the path enters natural forest, and the most rewarding section on the route starts here. Twenty minutes along the path there is a plaque denoting the beginning of the route up Newlands Ravine. Just south of this, the path crosses a scree belt at the foot of the ravine and seven minutes later meets the path from Newlands Forest just after crossing the stream in Els Ravine. The Contour Path continues through the forest, crossing another scree belt, and 20 minutes' walking beyond the Newlands Forest path meets a path left to Kirstenbosch via Lübberts Gift – part of the Silver Tree Trail.

At this point the Contour Path climbs about 100 m (the section is stepped with logs), at first skirting a scree belt filled with aloes, then crossing over the scree belt under a cliff before dropping again to its previous height. Thirty minutes later it meets a second path on the left from Kirstenbosch. Fifteen minutes further on, just beyond the waterfall, the Contour Path crosses Smuts' Track, the route up Skeleton Gorge (marked with a plaque). Beyond this the forest ends and the path traverses fynbos dominated by Waboom trees. Kirstenbosch is now visible below. You reach Nursery Ravine ten minutes after crossing Skeleton Gorge. The Contour Path continues above Kirstenbosch Reservoir to meet the path up Cecilia Ravine from Kirstenbosch 15 minutes later. The Contour Path continues towards some old gum trees which mark the beginning of Cecilia Forest, but you should take the path down to Kirstenbosch which leads to the top gate. The way through the gardens is well signposted.

2.2 CECILIA FOREST

A walk to Cecilia Ravine and Cecilia Forest from Kirstenbosch

Time: 2 ¾-3 hours.

Exertion: Moderate.

Height climbed: 400 m.

Start: Kirstenbosch top gate.

Route summary:
1. A moderate climb from the top gate of Kirsten-bosch to the Contour Path (20-25 minutes).
2. A moderate climb from the Contour Path to Cecilia Ravine (25-30 minutes).
3. A gentle stroll from Cecilia Ravine through the plantation to the Forestry Station (75 minutes).
4. A level walk from the Forestry Station to the junction of the Contour Path and the path through Kirstenbosch to the top gate (40 minutes).

Option: A shorter walk can be made by dropping down to the Contour Path from Cecilia Ravine.

Links: Constantia Nek (2,3).

Difficult terrain: None.

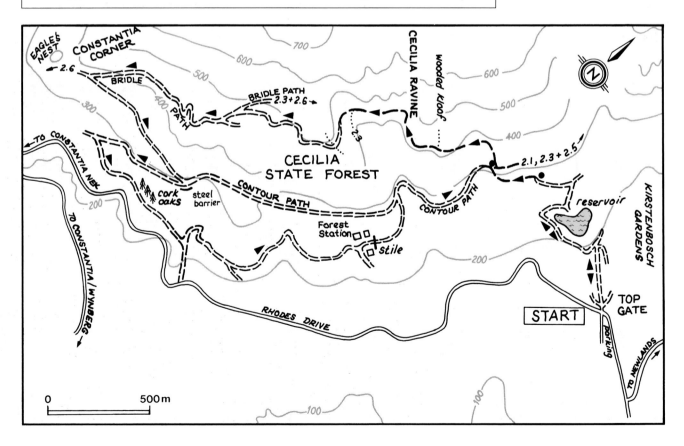

Apart from some climbing up the slopes above Kirstenbosch to Cecilia Ravine, this circuit is essentially a gentle ramble through the pine plantations of Cecilia Forest. It is a good route for a summer morning's hike when the initial short climb can be done early in the cool part of the day and the trees can shade you from the midday sun.

From the top gate of Kirstenbosch (there is a place to park on the other side of Rhodes Drive opposite the gate), follow the signs through the gardens to Cecilia Forest and Constantia Nek. The way leads past the Director's house on a paved road, skirting the east and south fences of the reservoir on a gravel road which comes to a dead end just beyond a sign reading 'Constantia Nek' and 'Contour Path'; the sign points to a path with log steps which leads to the Contour Path. To get from the top gate to the Contour Path takes 20-25 minutes of steady climbing.

Three metres to the right on the Contour Path a four-way sign shows the way up off the Contour Path to Cecilia Ravine on a path similarly paved with logs. This path leads up over a rise and then drops into a small forested kloof. From this kloof, the path climbs another rise dotted with Waboom trees (*Protea nitida*) before turning into Cecilia Ravine. The climb from the Contour Path to Cecilia Ravine takes 25-30 minutes.

In Cecilia Ravine – in the shade of the natural forest – the path passes a rockface covered with moss and ferns over which the stream flows to make an attractive pattern of small cascades. There are Tree ferns (*Cyathea capensis*) too.

Five minutes after leaving the ravine, a stepped path branches off to the right, past a small stream; take this path, rather than continuing on the level. (The other path winds down the south side of Cecilia Ravine and reaches the Contour Path in about 15 minutes. It is a convenient shortcut back to Kirstenbosch if necessary.)

The higher path leads shortly to the end of a gravel forestry road, which in turn leads into the pine plantation and meets a concreted section of the main forestry road from Constantia Nek to the reservoirs on the Back Table

Cecilia forest covers the eastern slopes of Table Mountain above Constantia Nek. Muizenberg Mountain rises above the flats to the south.

LEFT: *In August,* Podalyria *produce their sweetly-scented, pink flowers next to the path leading into the forest in Cecilia Ravine.*
RIGHT: *Tall trunks in the Cecilia pine plantations rise starkly above the dense litter of pine needles on the forest floor; a habitat where few indigenous plants survive.*

(the Bridle Path). Turn left (south) down this road, which runs through the plantation to a point close to a rocky outcrop called Eagle's Nest overlooking Constantia Nek, where the road continues to a dead end. Just short of this a sharp turn left heads back into the plantation and meets the Contour Path (joining from the left but not marked) at a steel barrier painted green and yellow. Continue on the extension of the Contour Path sharp right, into the forestry road which leads down to meet the gravel road running behind some private houses. Turn left along this road, which leads back through the plantation on the contour above Rhodes Drive to the Cecilia Forest Station. You will pass a copse of Cork oaks with their characteristic bark. Ignore both a track to the right from some abandoned forestry cottages to Rhodes Drive and, shortly after, an overgrown forestry road which branches to the right. The walk through the Cecilia plantation to the Forestry Station is an easy 75 minute stroll.

Continue through the Forest Station with the Forester's house on the right and service buildings on the left, over a low stile next to a metal gate. The road rises gently as it swings left to meet a forestry road from the left under some ancient blue gum trees. This is the Contour Path again, still not marked. Keep walking north up some log steps, and pass the fence on the boundary of Cecilia Forest and Kirstenbosch. You will shortly reach the point on the Contour Path where the Cecilia Ravine Path starts. The path to the right is the one back to the top gate of Kirstenbosch past the reservoir. It takes about 40 minutes to reach the top gate from the Cecilia Forest Station.

2.3 NURSERY RAVINE

A climb from Kirstenbosch up Nursery Ravine to Woodhead Reservoir and a walk down Cecilia Ravine

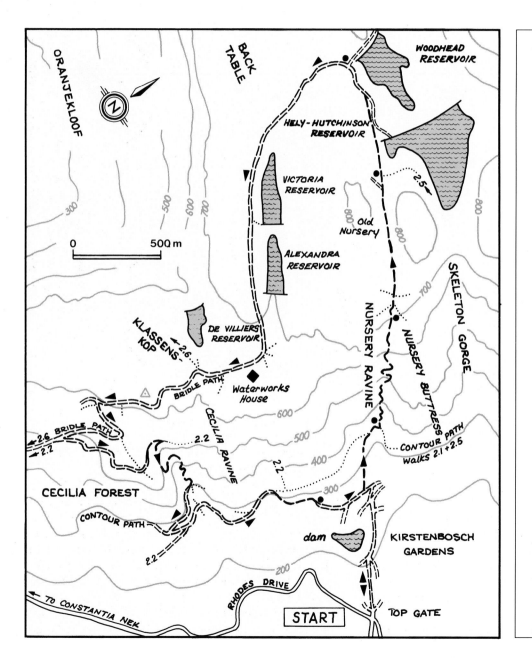

Time: 3 hours.

Exertion: High.

Height climbed: 650 m.

Start: Kirstenbosch top gate.

Route summary:
1. A moderate climb to the Contour Path, and along to Nursery Ravine (25 minutes).
2. A very steep climb up Nursery Ravine (55-60 minutes).
3. A gentle stroll from the top of Nursery Ravine, to Woodhead Reservoir (30 minutes).
4. A downhill walk on the Bridle Path to Cecilia Forest. Through the plantation to a path down the south side of Cecilia Ravine to a track to meet the Contour Path back to the start of the Cecilia Ravine Path (1 hour).
5. A downhill walk to the top gate of Kirstenbosch (10-15 minutes).

Links: Via the head of Skeleton Gorge to Maclear's Beacon (2.5); via Woodhead Reservoir to Kasteelspoort (1.3).

Difficult terrain: None.

The path up Nursery Ravine climbs steeply under the forest canopy before emerging under the cliffs of Castle Rock.

This is a circular route taking 3 hours' walking time, with a steep pull up Nursery Ravine but gentle walking thereafter. Because the really steep part of this route (up Nursery Ravine) is, for the most part, shaded by trees, it is popular even in summer. The whole route provides a lot of historic and natural interest. It passes through the site of the old Lister Nursery at Oudekraal at the head of Nursery Ravine (see page 88) and runs next to all five of the reservoirs on top of the mountain. From the man-made gardens in Kirstenbosch, the route traverses forest, fynbos and the plantations in Cecilia Forest.

Woodhead Reservoir, named after Sir John Woodhead, then mayor of Cape Town, was completed in 1897, ten years after the Woodhead Tunnel which carried water for Cape Town from Disa Kloof to the pipeline which ran from Slangolie Ravine to Kloof Nek. Hely-Hutchinson Reservoir, built in 1904, was named after the then governor, Sir Walter Hely-Hutchinson. Unlike modern dams which are constructed with cast reinforced concrete, the walls of these reservoirs were built of dressed stone. The construction of Woodhead Reservoir in Disa Gorge was a major undertaking. Excavations started in January 1893 and the dam wall was completed in 1897. By this time, work had also started on Hely-Hutchinson Reservoir above Woodhead Reservoir, to increase the water supply to Cape Town. An aerial cableway was built up Kasteelspoort with the lower terminus just above Victoria Road in Camps Bay. This carried supplies and sometimes workers up the mountain to the top of Kasteelspoort where a narrow-gauge railway carried the load to the construction sites. During the construction there was a small village complete with post office near the building sites to house the workers.

The concrete road from these dams down to Constantia Nek leads past the other three, smaller reservoirs before leaving the Back Table and entering the Cecilia Plantation. The Alexandra and Victoria reservoirs were constructed by the Wynberg Municipality in 1903, followed by De Villiers Reservoir in 1907.

This walk starts at the top gate of Kirstenbosch opposite which, across Rhodes Drive, there is a place to park, and also a bus stop. From the gate take the tarred road which becomes paved as it leads past the Director's house into the gardens, and follow the signs to the Contour Path and Nursery Ravine. These eventually lead you off a gravel track onto a short stretch of stepped path through the natural fynbos up to the Contour Path which can be reached after 25 minutes. A few metres to the right (north) along the Contour Path you enter the forested Nursery Ravine. Just across the stream is a low, old Department of Forestry plaque indicating the first stone steps leading up the ravine. The path leads steadily up the north side of the stream, stepped all the way, until, after climbing over some boulders, it leads out onto the slope below Castle Rock and zigzags up to and along the base of the cliffs. A short stretch along the stream is terminated by some boulders over which you clamber. Leave the ravine at another plaque

indicating Nursery Ravine. How long it takes you to climb the ravine from the Contour Path depends on your fitness, but 55-60 minutes is a reasonable time. In spring, growing in moist places at the top of the Nursery Ravine, you can find the rare Cape anemone (*Anemone tenuifolia*), the only representative in the Cape flora of a large genus of plants which is widespread in temperate regions in the northern hemisphere. The Cape anemone also grows on the Saddle.

At the top of Nursery Ravine, across the stream, a sign points to Kasteelspoort along a narrow path. Take this path which follows a small valley bordered by some interesting rocks, which have been eroded into fantastic shapes. In this valley there are the ruins of some buildings which mark the site of the old nursery (more a trial plot of plantation trees) which gave the ravine its name. Beyond some rocks at the head of this valley, Woodhead and Hely-Hutchinson reser-

voirs come into view. The path leads straight down past felled pines to a sign indicating Skeleton Gorge and Maclear's Beacon to the right and Kasteelspoort ahead. Carry straight on along the path which becomes a stone paved track. This soon meets the concrete road which, to the right, runs under the wall of the Hely-Hutchinson Reservoir. Follow the concrete road to the left for 50 m or so to a sign at the wall of Woodhead Reservoir. From the top of Nursery Ravine to the Woodhead Reservoir wall is a gentle 30-minute stroll, well deserved after the climb up the ravine. For those who wish to link up with other routes,

FAR LEFT: *The Cape Anemone,* Anemone tenuifolia, *can be seen at the top of Nursery Ravine and on the Saddle during the winter months.* CENTRE: *Pines, felled to restore the natural fynbos, litter the slopes above Hely-Hutchinson Reservoir.* BELOW: *Logs help to prevent erosion.*

THE LISTER NURSERY

Lichen-covered Turkey oaks, Quercus cerris, *at the site of the old Lister Nursery.*

Nursery Ravine above Kirstenbosch, one of the popular routes up Table Mountain, takes its name from an old forestry nursery which was established in the shallow valley at its head: Oudekraal.

Whereas the reason for forestry plantations now is the ever-increasing demand for timber and pulp, a major rationale for their establishment last century was to increase water runoff in catchment areas. It is now conclusively demonstrated that the indigenous vegetation, *properly conserved*, is more efficient for this purpose, but the mountains of the south-western Cape are still littered with plantations of alien, sometimes invasive tree species whose economic viability is also questionable. Table Mountain is no exception.

In 1884, in the spirit of the times, Joseph Storr Lister, Superintendant of Plantations at Cape Town, appointed a forester, Paul Schickerdanz, as Forest Guard for Table Mountain and gave him the task of establishing a nursery for exotic plantation trees at Oudekraal. Access to the site was provided by Thomas Charles John Bain, son of Andrew Geddes Bain, who built the Bain's Kloof Pass between Wellington and Ceres. He laid out the Bridle Path which provided a route to the Back Table with gentle gradients for horses. In Ash Valley, just to the south of Oudekraal, where the Western Province Mountain Club hut now stands, a stone cottage was built for Paul Schickerdanz, as were barracks for 15 convict labourers.

Several different species of trees were propagated at Oudekraal, including Blackwood (*Acacia melanoxylon*), Silver birch (*Betula pendula*), fir trees (*Chamaecyparis lawsoniana, Cryptomeria japonica* and *Cupressus* species), pines (*Pinus radiata*), ash (*Fraxinus* spp), elm (*Ulmas procera*) and Turkey oaks (*Quercus cerris*).

Some of the plantations established near the nursery were inundated by the Hely-Hutchinson Reservoir; the rest, together with self-sown pine trees, have been felled recently, leaving a mass of logs in the area. At the site of the old nursery, however, one can still see ancient *Cryptomerias*, one now on its side, together with Turkey oaks and Silver birch. The invasive species have been removed and replaced by indigenous trees – Yellowwoods (*Podocarpus* spp), Rooiels (*Cunonia capensis*), Cape beech (*Rapanea melanophloeos*) and others.

the sign shows the way to Kasteelspoort across the reservoir wall – from here it is a walk of five minutes to the Overseer's cottage and the sign to Kasteelspoort. (It is sobering to realise just how fast one can cross the Peninsula by walking up Kasteelspoort, across the mountain, and down Nursery Ravine.)

From the southern end of the Woodhead Reservoir wall, take the concrete road south from the sign indicating the direction of Constantia Nek. The road leads past the Alexandra and Victoria reservoirs on the left, passes the stone Overseer's cottage on the edge of the mountain above Cecilia Ravine and, on the right, De Villiers Reservoir sited at the eastern head of Orange Kloof, with a fine view of Grootkop on the other side. The road descends steeply down the eastern slopes and runs along the top of Cecilia Forest to a dead end, which is the turning place for municipal vehicles unable to negotiate the very sharp turn back left into the plantation at a steel gate. Take the sharp turn back into the plantation. The road zigzags down the slope: where it meets a track, turn sharp left, eventually emerging on the northern side of the plantation. At this point a path follows the edge of the plantation down the slope; do not take this, however, as it is steep, loose and badly eroded. Instead, continue on the concrete road back and sharp right into the plantation. The concrete paving stops and the road becomes a sand track; further along there is another short stretch of concrete paving. At this point take a branch track leading off left. This leads north and peters out at the edge of the plantation to become a path, now on shale, which winds down and comes to a T-junction with the path from Cecilia Ravine. Take the right-hand branch, which zigzags down the slope, crossing and re-crossing two streams and eventually becoming a forestry track next to some blue gum trees. This track runs south and meets a track above the Cecilia Forest Station. Turn left on this – the Contour Path here is just another forestry track from Constantia Nek. Continue north (left) on the Contour Path, to the boundary of Cecilia Forest, passing the intersection withh forestry track from Cecilia Forest Station, and Kirstenbosch, just beyond which (on the Contour Path) is a four-way sign indicating Cecilia Ravine to the left and Kirstenbosch to the right. From Woodhead Reservoir to this point takes about 1 hours.

Fifteen minutes' walk past the lower fence of Kirstenbosch Reservoir through the well-signposted garden will bring you back to the top gate.

Erica curviflora *flowers in the shallow valley of the old Lister Nursery.*

2.4 NEWLANDS RAVINE

An ascent of Newlands Ravine from Newlands Forest and a walk around Devil's Peak on the Top Contour Path, King's Blockhouse Path and the Contour Path

Time: 4¾ hours.

Exertion: High.

Height climbed: 650 m.

Start: The concrete path which leaves the south-west corner of the intersection of Rhodes Drive with Edinburgh Drive.

Route summary:

1. A fairly steep climb through Newlands Forest to the Contour Path (45 minutes).

2. A level walk on the Contour Path to Newlands Ravine Path (10 minutes).

3. A very steep zigzag climb up Newlands Ravine (50 minutes).

4. A downhill walk to Breakfast Rock (20 minutes).

5. A level walk along the Top Contour Path which finally drops steeply to join the path to the King's Blockhouse (55 minutes).

6. A level walk to the King's Blockhouse (20 minutes).

7. A short, steep drop from King's Blockhouse to a track to the Contour Path, which is a level walk back to the junction with the path to Newlands Forest (45 minutes).

8. A steep climb down Newlands Forest to the start (30-35 minutes).

Links: The Upper Contour Path (1.5); Devil's Peak (1.1); the Contour Path south (2.1).

Difficult terrain: Shortly after Breakfast Rock, the Top Contour Path crosses a wide, safe ledge with a steep drop below.

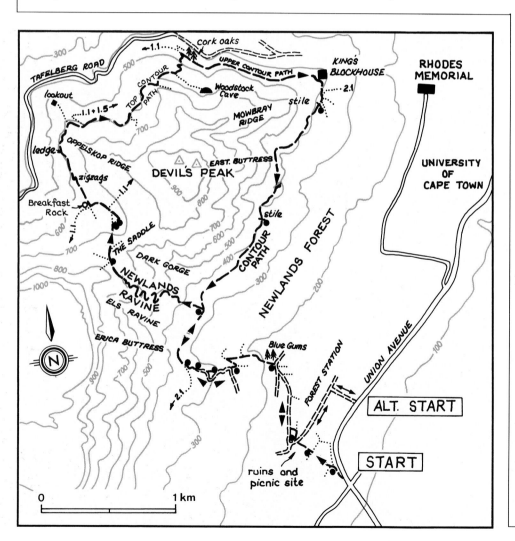

Between Devil's Peak and Erica Buttress on the eastern face of Table Mountain there are three steep parallel gorges. Of these, only the centre one, Newlands Ravine, provides a safe route up to the Saddle. Els Gorge and Dark Gorge neighbouring Newlands Ravine are extremely steep and dangerous and should on no account be attempted. The only routes up onto the Eastern Table of Table Mountain from the Saddle are rock-climbing routes; the easiest (the Ledges Route) is rated a C climb; this should not be undertaken without guidance and the necessary skills and proper equipment.

Newlands Ravine is one of the 'musts' for walkers. This circular route combines forest and fynbos with spectacular views of the whole of Cape Town and the historical interest of the blockhouses. The Newlands Ravine Path starts from the Contour Path a few minutes' walk north past the scree belt where the Contour Path crosses the bed of Newlands Ravine. There are as many ways to reach this point as there are routes to the Contour Path, but a convenient starting point is Newlands Forest. Here, there is a confusing network of forest tracks, recognised paths and *ad hoc* paths as this is a favourite place for walkers, joggers and bergies. The route to the Contour Path described here is, therefore, by no means unique, but it is reasonably straightforward and signposted in places.

Newlands Forest is managed by the Cape Town City

Moss glows in the dappled sunlight below the trees in the forest along the contour Path near Newlands Ravine.

Council and includes old pine and blue gum plantations in addition to the natural forest (now invaded more or less seriously with alien trees) on the higher slopes and in the kloofs. The value of maintaining the plantations is questionable. Before the settlement of the Cape by the Dutch East India Company, these slopes were covered with Afromontane forest and it would be ecologically satisfying should the plantations, when felled at maturity (some of the trees are long past their prime), be replaced with indigenous pioneer species in order ultimately to extend the natural forest to this area.

The concrete path which runs parallel to the Cape Town-bound lane of the M3 dual-carriageway (Union Avenue), beginning at the Rhodes Avenue intersection, provides a convenient start to the walk. A few metres up the path, steps lead off at an angle to the left at a Municipality notice depicting what is and is not allowed in the forest. This leads to the boundary fence where there is a sign reading 'Table Mountain/Tafelberg' and a sign warning, 'Do not walk or jog alone'. The latter sign should be taken seriously, particularly by women, as there have been several rapes and attempted rapes in this area during the last few years. (This point can also be reached by a short path from Union Avenue where it swings right.) Ignore the path to the left and continue up to an open area under the oaks where the ruins of some old brick reservoirs are prominent and the path meets a gravel forestry road. This road provides a third access to this route from the Newlands Forestry Station gate; it is the left-hand branch of the T-junction which is met by the road through the Forestry Station as it clears the buildings.

Across the gravel road from the reservoir ruins a path leads up some steps into the plantation at a sign reading 'Table Mountain'. Some 50 m along this path, take the path which heads directly up the slope under the pines; this shortly meets a gravel forestry road. Turn right along the road, which some way up the slope meets another road, at an angle and a few metres beyond the junction of another path from the right. A few metres to the right beyond the junction, under blue gum trees, a path leads steeply up

TOP LEFT: *The plaque in memory of forester Frank Jarman is situated just below the King's Blockhouse.* LEFT: *The sign which indicates the start of the Newlands Ravine path can be seen clearly next to the Contour Path.*
RIGHT: *The rocks at the top of Newlands Ravine frame the urban sprawl on the Cape Flats far below.*

The Cork oaks which stand to the east of the junction of the Top Contour Path and the path from Tafelberg Road to the King's Blockhouse.

some more steps at a sign reading 'Contour Path'. This path continues up the slope on one side of a kloof and is joined, under some oaks, by a broad path leading up some steps from the right, before coming to a T-junction. The right-hand branch crosses the stream bed in the kloof; ignore this, however, and take the left-hand branch, which turns sharply back left and ascends some stone steps to another T-junction. Here turn right up the slope to a forestry road at a sign reading 'Contour Path'. As the road swings left, the path leading up leaves it at another 'Contour Path' sign to the right, effectively cutting a corner on the road, which is met again just before it comes to a dead end. From this point, at another 'Contour Path' sign, the stepped path climbs steeply to meet the Contour Path. At the junction, note the 'Newlands Forest' sign and the Cape Town City Council signboard a few metres away for the return route. The climb up to the Contour Path takes 45 minutes.

At the Contour Path, turn right (north). The path crosses two stream beds in the natural forest before coming to the tumbled rocks of the scree belt in Newlands Ravine itself. The path up Newlands Ravine leaves the Contour Path in the forest beyond (north of) the scree belt and is marked by a low sign reading 'Newlands Ravine' at its start. It takes 10 minutes to walk along the Contour Path from the Newlands Forest path to the start of Newlands Ravine.

At first, the path climbs on stone steps, zigzagging up the slope in the soft, deep shade under the trees, the only sound coming from the occasional forest bird, heard but not seen. Higher up the slope under the rock buttress, the path emerges from the trees for a stretch and here, after a fire, Painted ladies (*Gladiolus carneus*) flower the following spring. After the path clears the last patch of trees, it zigzags across the ravine over the scree past unsightly but necessary anti-erosion fences erected to deter shortcuts. The higher reaches of Newlands Ravine are not forested and the steep slope and the scree may be the reason. Higher still, the path heads straight up the kloof on rock steps and then abruptly reaches the top at a signpost that reads 'Newlands Ravine Footpath'. The climb up Newlands Ravine is steep and strenuous but only takes 50 minutes.

Only a super-fit Spartan would not stop here to regain his breath, congratulate himself, and admire the view down the ravine. At the top there is a confusion of minor paths. Take the main path which leads down in a northerly direction through a dense patch of *Protea lepidocarpoden-dron* to a signpost pointing back to 'Newlands Ravine' at a crossroad, and here turn right to another 'Newlands Ravine' signpost close by at a second crossroad. Ahead is one of the firebreak tracer belts straight up Devil's Peak and to the right a path to the top of Dark Gorge. Take the path left, however, which leads along the north side of the stream to Breakfast Rock – reached 20 minutes after leaving the top of Newlands Ravine. This is a favourite place to stop, since it provides some shelter and is at the junction of three paths (the other two being the Saddle Path from Tafelberg Road or the Upper Contour Path on the north face of Table Mountain, and the Top Contour Path).

The Top Contour Path leaves Breakfast Rock on its north-eastern side and initially heads in a northerly direction down two small zigzags to the elevation where it passes under the cliffs on Oppelskop Ridge over a wide ledge with a steep drop below. The ledge should not pose any problems. Oppelskop itself comes into view as the path turns towards the north face of Devil's Peak. There is a path leading off the Top Contour Path to the abandoned forestry lookout on Oppelskop, from which there are fine views of Table Mountain and the city below. A few steps along the Top Contour Path another path leads sharp left back down the slope in what is the first of a series of zigzags to the Upper Contour Path. The Top Contour Path continues into the kloof between Oppelskop Ridge and Blockhouse Ridge, running more or less parallel to the Upper Contour Path, which is visible below. In the kloof it passes the start of a steep, faint path which zigzags up to Minor Peak. As it rounds Blockhouse Ridge, the path starts to drop steeply down the slope on stone steps. At this point, a faint path continues on the contour. Take the path down, which shortly joins a path from the right to Woodstock Cave and drops, through a series of zigzags, to a junction some 30 m to the north-west of a grove of Cork oaks. At this junction, which is reached 55 minutes after leaving Breakfast Rock,

turn sharp right towards the trees on a wide path. This path comes from the spot where Tafelberg Road and the Upper Contour Path meet. Ignore the path which continues down the slope.

On the slopes below are the restored remains of the Queen's Blockhouse, once called the York Blockhouse and one of three fortifications built by the British after they captured the Cape from the Dutch in 1795. These fortifications extended the southern defensive lines of Cape Town up the slopes of Devil's Peak against infantry attack. The ruins of the Prince of Wales' Blockhouse lie below, further to the east and just above De Waal Drive. The King's Blockhouse, a National Monument, stands on Mowbray Ridge directly above Rhodes Memorial. The path through the Cork oaks leads directly to this blockhouse, and is a level walk of 20 minutes. At the King's Blockhouse two old cannon, their barrels stopped with cement, point their muzzles at the vast expanse of buildings and roads below – a vastly different scene to that when they still served a purpose. Between the cannon there is a plaque in memory of the forester, Frank Jarman, who at the end of last century lived just below the blockhouse (which then served as a jail for the convict forestry labour). It reads, 'He found these barren stoney slopes treeless, and left them covered with forest.' There is no doubt that at the time these slopes did appear barren, but the results of this noble sentiment and those good intentions can be seen in the tangle of exotic invasive alien trees which now mars the upper slopes of the Groote Schuur Estate.

A steep, badly eroded path leads down from beside the eastern cannon below the blockhouse to a gravel road. Turn right (south) on this road, which shortly leads to a stile which marks the boundary of the Groote Schuur Estate, and is signposted as such. Once through the stile, two paths face you; the top path is the Contour Path, which climbs gently at first, then levels out amongst the alien trees past First and Second Waterfall ravines on the slopes of Devil's Peak to reach the second stile which marks the southern boundary of the Groote Schuur Estate. This is reached 20 minutes after leaving the King's Blockhouse. Beyond this stile, the Contour Path enters natural forest (in which is the start of the Newlands Ravine Path) and crosses the scree slope and two stream beds, reaching the junction with the signposted path from Newlands Forest after another 25 minutes' walk.

To reach the start, retrace the route down through Newlands Forest – a walk of 30-35 minutes.

2.5 SMUTS' TRACK

An ascent of Skeleton Gorge and climb to Maclear's Beacon, returning by way of Nursery Ravine

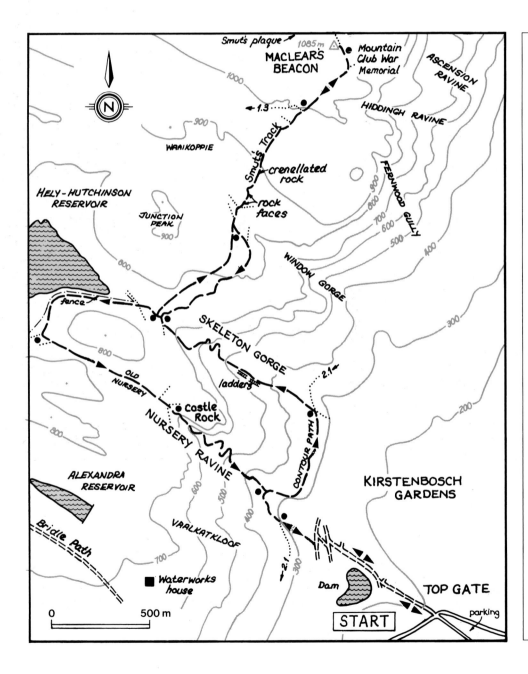

Time: 5¼ hours.

Exertion: Very high.

Height climbed: 950 m.

Start: The top gate of Kirstenbosch.

Route summary:
1. A moderate climb to the Contour Path from the top gate of Kirstenbosch (25 minutes).
2. A level walk north along the Contour Path to Skeleton Gorge (15 minutes).
3. A steep climb up Skeleton Gorge (1 hour).
4. A moderate climb from the top of Skeleton Gorge up two easy rock faces to Maclear's Beacon (65 to 70 minutes).
5. An easy walk down to the top of Skeleton Gorge (50 minutes).
6. A level walk past Hely-Hutchinson Reservoir, through the old nursery at Oudekraal, to the top of Nursery Ravine (30 to 35 minutes).
7. A steep, stepped descent of Nursery Ravine to the Contour Path (45 minutes).
8. A moderate downhill walk from the Contour Path through Kirstenbosch (20 minutes).

Option: Return to Kirstenbosch down Skeleton Gorge (70 minutes).

Links: Platteklip Gorge from Maclear's Beacon (1.3); Kasteelspoort (1.6) and the Bridle Path (2.3) via Woodhead Reservoir; the Contour Path (2.1).

Difficult terrain: In the higher reaches of Skeleton Gorge there are two fixed wooden ladders and a chain to help you up some steep rocks; you scramble up other rocks with the aid of tree roots as handholds.

A small but dense stand of the Everlasting, Helichrysum patulum, *marks the top of Skeleton Gorge.*

Because the route of this walk has been extended to include a descent of Nursery Ravine, it is more convenient to start at the top gate of Kirstenbosch and park opposite it in Klaassens Road. There is a slightly shorter alternative route through a different section of the gardens from the kiosk and restaurant which is well signposted 'Skeleton Gorge'. All the ravines north of Skeleton Gorge on the east face of Table Mountain are very steep and difficult rock climbs, very dangerous for the unequipped and unskilled. Therefore keep to the route.

Maclear's Beacon, the highest point on the Peninsula, can be reached by means of a variety of routes, but this route follows Smuts' favourite walk up Table Mountain. It traverses three of the characteristic veld types on the mountain, namely the forest in the kloofs, the dense fynbos of the Back Table and the short restio and erica communities of the Front Table. It is a sustained climb almost all the way to the top and demands a certain degree of fitness to match that of the grand old man who gave his name to this route.

ABOVE: *The sign on the Contour Path showing the way up Skeleton Gorge.* LEFT: *In the higher reaches of Skeleton Gorge, exposed roots provide handholds to pull you up the rocks.* RIGHT ABOVE: *The Arum Lily,* Zantedeschia aethiopica, *is common in the stream bed in Skeleton Gorge and elsewhere in damp spots on Table Mountain.*

From the top gate, follow the signs indicating 'Contour Path' and 'Nursery Ravine' which lead past the Director's house and the protea section up to the natural vegetation above the gardens. A gravel track bears right, then swings sharp left. A short way up this arm, a sign points to 'Nursery Ravine' up a stepped path which leads to the Contour Path. The walk through the gardens to the Contour Path takes 25 minutes.

Turn right on the Contour Path where there is a sign indicating the direction of Skeleton Gorge and continue into and out of the forest in Nursery Ravine, passing the path up the ravine and continuing around the slopes under Castle Rock into the forest in Skeleton Gorge. Just before the stream bed there is a sign at path level indicating 'Smuts' Track' at the start of the broad stepped climb up the gorge. From Nursery Ravine to Skeleton Gorge takes just 15 minutes on the Contour Path.

Smuts' Track climbs steadily up the gorge through the forest on a path (always on the left or south side of the stream) stepped with stones or logs. Higher up, the gradient

increases until the path reaches the first of two wooden ladders, placed to help you up a short section of steep rocks with no handholds. Roots, now polished by thousands of hands, are almost uncannily placed to help you up the following rock scramble. A fixed chain also helps. The path runs under the trunk of an uprooted tree before climbing the tumbled rocks in the stream bed itself next to the vertical face of a large rock. Below a dry stone wall, retained by wire meshing and topped with barbed wire, built across the stream, the path turns right out of the kloof and zigzags twice up the slope, passing under an overhanging and unstable-looking cliff on the right. Redwinged Starlings nest in holes in this cliff; in early summer, the demanding tweets of nestlings add to the song of the forest birds which accompanies the climb. Beyond the cliff, the path crosses the stream bed to its left (south) side as it emerges from the trees. Shortly after, the path splits around a boulder; take the right-hand branch, which leads straight to a small old sign reading 'Skeleton Gorge' at the junction with a path to the right. Note this path – which on this walk is used on

A distant view to Woodhead Reservoir and the tops of the Twelve Apostles from Smuts' Track.

GENERAL JAN CHRISTIAAN SMUTS

Mountain Club of South Africa

General Jan Christiaan Smuts was a keen and active member of the Mountain Club of South Africa and was often seen striding out high on Table Mountain, staff in hand, well into his old age. Smuts' attitude towards the mountain was reverential and best summed up in his address to a gathering at Maclear's Beacon on 25 February 1923 at the unveiling of the Mountain Club War Memorial for members who had died in service during World War I, from which I quote:

'To them the true church where they worshipped was Table Mountain. Table Mountain was their cathedral where they heard a subtler music and saw wider visions and were inspired with a loftier spirit. Here in life they breathed the great air; here in death their memory will fill the upper spaces. 'The Mountain is not merely something externally sublime. It has a great historic and spiritual meaning for us.'

Today, Smuts' love of the mountain is recalled in the name of one of his favourite walks, the route up Skeleton Gorge to Maclear's Beacon – Smuts' Track.

the return – but continue straight on for a few metres to a signpost showing the direction of Kasteelspoort and Maclear's Beacon (right). Depending on your fitness, the ascent of Skeleton Gorge takes about an hour. Skeleton Gorge is not as steep a climb as Nursery Ravine.

The path in the direction of Maclear's Beacon from the signpost may or may not be Smuts' Track; the lower path from the old sign (a larger, better used path) may have that distinction. The higher path is interesting, however, in that it leads through a stand of wet fynbos, dominated by the tall, straggly White daisy *Osmotopsis asteriscoides* and the crimson-flowered *Erica curviflora*, which form dense stands here and provide a richly coloured scene when flowering together at the beginning of summer. The path heads straight up the slope and over the rise to join the lower path a few metres beyond a signpost on the latter indicating 'Maclear's Beacon' and 'Skeleton Gorge'. The joint path drops to cross the stream above Window Gorge and continues up the other side straight towards a rock face. From the stream, two other minor paths approach the rock face to the left of the main path. Don't take these, as the routes up the face are not clear and not easy. On the main path there is an easy way up the rock face left up a wide cleft and over two low ledges to a cairn. Beyond the cairn the path crosses a sandy patch to a second rock face where it swings left up an easily climbed cleft to another cairn.

Cairns lead you up through the rocks above the second rock face, the path heading directly towards a large rock which looks like the crenellated tower of a medieval castle. This is passed on the left as the path clears the rocks to emerge onto a sandy area where the path from Woodhead Reservoir joins from the left at a signpost indicating 'Kasteelspoort/Blinkwater Ravine' to the left and 'Maclear's Beacon/Platteklip Gorge' straight on. After climbing through a low rock band, the path reaches the plateau surrounding the rocky platform on which the large stone cairn of Maclear's Beacon was built. There is a profusion of paths in this area, one leading to the right around the platform to its north side where, below Maclear's Beacon, a plaque in honour of General Smuts has been let into the rock. The Mountain Club War Memorial is a metal disc set horizontally on a rock on the platform to the east of Maclear's Beacon. Just below this, to the south-east, a signpost indicates the direction of Skeleton Gorge. The climb from the top of Skeleton Gorge to Maclear's Beacon takes 65-70 minutes.

Start the return from the signpost indicating the path to

Skeleton Gorge. On the return route, note that the way down through the rocks is well marked with stone cairns, and directly above each easy descent of the two rock faces there is an obvious cairn. Below the second, take the main, left-most path. Over the stream above Window Gorge, take the main path past the signpost, not the right-hand branch a few metres before it (i.e. the path used on the way up). The main path runs closer to the edge of the mountain, at a slightly lower elevation, to the old 'Skeleton Gorge' sign at the top of the gorge. The return journey takes about 50 minutes.

At the top of Skeleton Gorge, walk a few metres to the right to the signpost showing the direction of Kasteel-spoort. This path leads through some Keurboom trees (*Virgilia oroboides*) to a very sandy area at a corner of the fence around Hely-Hutchinson Reservoir. The path bears left alongside the fence and follows the direction of the fence as it turns first southwest then south. As the fence reaches a corner and swings west, the path drops down a rocky slope and meets, at a signpost, the path to Woodhead Reservoir from the top of Nursery Ravine. Turn left here in the direction of 'Nursery Ravine'. From a very sandy slope with a bad erosion channel on the left, the path drops into the site of the old nursery where Turkey oaks (*Quercus cerris*), birch (*Betula pendula*) and ancient *Cryptomeria japonica* trees still grow along the path. From here, the path continues west to a signpost at the head of Nursery Ravine, 35 minutes from Skeleton Gorge.

At the signpost turn left across the stream bed to the steep left (north) side of the ravine. A few metres further on, at a low sign which reads 'Keep to footpath', the path down Nursery Ravine drops steeply off a minor path (which continues along the edge before climbing up Castle Rock). The path down Nursery Ravine drops steeply on rock steps under the vertical face of Castle Rock, zigzags twice, then enters the forest in the ravine where the steep descent continues on rock or log steps, always on the left (north) side of the stream bed.

At one point, the path may appear to cross the stream at a small stone cairn, but in fact turns right, then left, past a big boulder. The Contour Path is reached gratefully after 45 minutes of continuous stepping down. Here turn right and, just after crossing a subsidiary stream bed, take the path signposted 'Top Gate' down off the Contour Path to Kirstenbosch Botanic gardens. Follow the 'Top Gate' signs through the gardens to arrive at the start of the walk 20 minutes after leaving Nursery Ravine.

Aristea major, *the largest of several aristeas on the Peninsula, flowers in summer in a recent burn alongside Smuts' Track.*

2.6 BEL OMBRE

An ascent of Bel Ombre from Constantia Nek via Eagle's Nest and Constantia Corner and a return via De Villiers Reservoir and the Bridle Path

Time: 2¾-3 hours.

Exertion: Moderate.

Height climbed: 550 m.

Start: The gate at the start of the Bridle Path under the pine trees on the north side of Constantia Nek.

Route summary:
1. A steep climb from Constantia Nek up onto Constantia Corner ridge (1 hour).

2. A moderate climb up onto Bel Ombre (25 minutes).
3. A largely downhill walk down the north side of Bel Ombre to De Villiers Reservoir (25 minutes).
4. A steady downhill walk along the Bridle Path and path from Eagle's Nest to the start (55-60 minutes).

Links: Woodhead Reservoir via the Bridle Path (2.3); Kirstenbosch via Cecilia Ravine (2.2).

Difficult terrain: The path up Constantia Corner is very steep in places and involves some rock scrambling, but no exposure. At one point on the south-facing rock band of Bel Ombre there is a short climb up a rock with good handholds above a short drop where the ledge is somewhat narrow.

RIGHT: *Mimetes fimbriifolius is a prominent feature of the fynbos on the Peninsula and several trees are evident above the Bridle Path below the De Villiers Reservoir.*

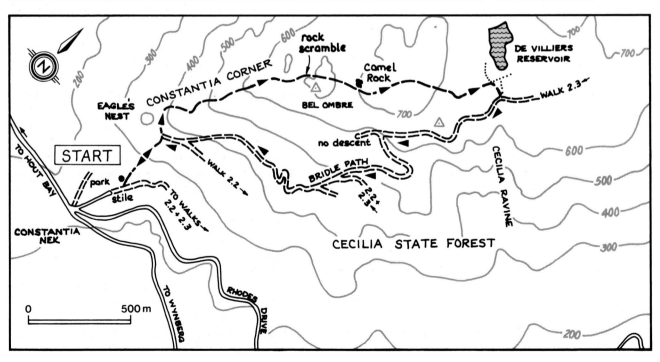

The path up Bel Ombre parallels the Bridle Path, but at a higher elevation, revealing fine views of Orange Kloof, the back of Grootkop and the southern Twelve Apostles.

The route starts at Constantia Nek, where there is parking under the pines next to the private houses. Cross the stile next to the gate at the start of the Bridle Path and take the stepped path marked 'Back Table' which leads up fairly steeply through the plantation. Only fanatical dog-lovers will enjoy this stretch: it is a popular walk for dogs and the smell of their droppings is overwhelming. The path winds up through the plantation and then next to it until it meets a forestry track. Turn left along the track to its end, where several paths lead up to a nek next to Eagle's Nest – take the zigzag path to avoid erosion. At the nek, take the path which leads north up to the rocks, then bears left, becoming steep and badly eroded in sandy areas and passing through a thick stand of proteas. The path passes next to a vertical rock face, then turns straight up the steep slope just before an erosion gully. On this slope the path is not always clear, but follow the stone cairns on the right-hand side of

the gully, crossing over a small rock band up to a second rock band where the path (now clearly visible on a very steep slope) crosses the gully and swings back to the base of some rocks up which you scramble through a deep cleft. The path swings to the right under some rocks and then left over them up to the ridge on top of Constantia Corner. At the top of the ridge there are views of the backs of the Twelve Apostles to the west over Orange Kloof to Grootkop, and to the east out over the Cape Flats to False Bay and the southern Hottentots Holland Mountains. While I enjoyed this vista one day, a pair of Rock Kestrels floated past at my elevation, riding the thermals in search of prey. The route up Constantia Corner is steep and takes one hour. The path is badly eroded (because of sandy soil on a steep slope) and every care should be taken not to make matters worse. The plant cover has disappeared because thousands of hikers' boots have exposed the soil to wash-away in heavy rains, and such a path rapidly becomes an erosion gully.

The ridge on Constantia Corner leads straight to the rather daunting faces of Bel Ombre. At the cliffs, the path

swings left, then up through the rocks. At one spot, the path narrows over a sheer but short fall from where there is a short climb up through a cleft in the rocks with good handholds. The rest of the climb up Bel Ombre is plain sailing on a clear path through another cleft in the rocks to the top, but not actually to the beacon, as this is a little way to the right. The top of Bel Ombre is a flattish, very rocky area reminiscent of the top of Constantiaberg, which is clearly visible not far to the south. It is well worth your while to explore the surroundings here, particularly for the fine views into Orange Kloof and towards Table Mountain.

From the top of Bel Ombre follow the stone cairns down north through the rocks, passing between two huge boulders into a small valley and up the other side to the fantastically shaped Camel Rock. Ignore a path which heads off to the right and eventually links up with the Bridle Path. Camel Rock looks like something in a Dali painting: camel-like only from the south, it is even more weirdly formed when viewed from the north. From Camel Rock the path passes through another rock cleft before dropping onto and over a small sandy plateau and down to De Villiers Reservoir where it meets the concrete Bridle Path. Water is available from a tap at the Overseer's cottage.

Turn right onto the concrete road and follow it down on the steep eastern slopes. The damp, shaded seepage slopes above the road are rich in plants, including disas. The concrete road drops down next to the pine plantation to a padlocked barrier just before a sharp turn left. Straight on, the road becomes a turning spot because vehicles cannot make the tight bend. Do not take the path which leads back to Eagle's Nest from here: this path splits, and thereafter both paths are badly eroded, and both end at a steep, loose rock face. Rather continue on the forestry road into the plantation (the Bridle Path) and follow it down, always keeping right at intersections, until the path emerges from the plantation and ends in the cul de sac below Eagle's Nest. From here take the stepped path on which you started out back to Constantia Nek. The walk down from De Villiers Reservoir can be made easily in less than one hour.

TOP RIGHT: *The fantastically-shaped Camel Rock stands on a ridge just north of Bel Ombre.* RIGHT: *These homerias are toxic to stock.* LEFT: *The moist slopes on Constantia Corner are a delight in spring when myriads of yellow* Spiloxene *flower. Hout Bay and Karbonkelberg lie to the south.*

CHAPTER 3

HOUT BAY

FAR LEFT: *The Sentinel stands guard over Hout Bay far below the vantage point above the manganese mine workings.*
LEFT: Geissorhiza aspera *grows in wet crevices on the west facing slopes above Hout Bay.*

Hout Bay's recorded history is almost as long as that of Cape Town. Jan van Riebeeck, the first commander of the Dutch East India Company settlement at the Cape, early on sent a group of his men to explore the area surrounding the bay, which by then must have been a familiar sight to the ships rounding the Cape. The explorers found a wooded valley, which was soon exploited to satisfy the early settlement's demand for timber – the same great appetite which virtually denuded the slopes of Table Mountain; it was probably only the distance from Cape Town and the difficulty of reaching the area which protected the higher reaches of Hout Bay from the same fate. Today, this area – Orange Kloof – is a nature reserve, closed to the general public, to conserve what is now the largest, richest area of unspoilt Afromontane forest on the Peninsula.

The Hout Bay valley and bay are surrounded by mountains. The scenic splendour of this area arises from the way these fall steeply into the sea or to the valley bottom. The peaks from Constantiaberg to Chapman's Peak which form the eastern arm of the bay are, with the exception of the two named, really the slightly uplifted edge of the plateau which makes up most of the western side of the Silvermine Nature Reserve. Constantiaberg is much higher than the plateau; Chapman's Peak and Lower Chapman's Peak, although lower, stand apart from it. Disa Kloof and, below it, Orange Kloof are bounded by Bel Ombre on the east, the Back Table and, on the west, the last of the Twelve Apostles and Grootkop. The massif which forms the western arm of the bay, with Karbonkelberg its highest peak, is separated from the Twelve Apostles by a low nek. On the northern side of Suther Peak above Llandudno Bay is Little Lion's Head, quite unlike a lion from any angle but very similar to Lion's Head itself.

There is a striking resemblance between the slopes of the mountains on the east of Hout Bay and the slopes of the Blousteenberge on the east of Kogel Bay in False Bay. Both are made up of a conglomerate type of soil with rounded pebbles embedded in decomposed shale (at one time the bottom of the sea or vast lake) overlaid with Table Mountain sandstone. On the eastern slopes above both these bays there are outcroppings of a manganese-bearing rock. A unique pincushion, *Leucospermum cordatum*, is found growing only in a limited area around the manganese outcrop of the slopes above Kogel Bay, but I am not aware of any unique plant species near Hout Bay.

Tens of thousands of visitors motor along Chapman's Peak Drive to view the spectacular scenery of Hout Bay, but anyone prepared to walk this area will reap far greater rewards. This chapter comprises three walks on the eastern side of Hout Bay and the walk up Karbonkelberg which, in terms of scenery and plant life, is exceptional.

3.1 CONSTANTIABERG TRAVERSE

A walk from Constantia Nek over Vlakkenberg Nek to the western slopes of Constantiaberg and down to the abandoned manganese mine above Hout Bay

Time: 3¼ hours.

Height climbed: 350 m.

Exertion: Light.

Start: At a sign reading 'Pedestrian Access to Vlakkenberg Hiking Trail' 100 m down the Hout Bay road from Constantia Nek.

Route summary:
1. A steady climb from Constantia Nek to Vlakkenberg Nek (50 minutes).
2. An easy walk down to Bokkemanskloof Stream and up to join the tarred road up Constantiaberg (65 minutes).
3. From the tarred road a gently dropping traverse of the western of Constantiaberg to the old manganese mine above Hout Bay (50 minutes).
4. A short, fairly steep zig-zag walk down to the forestry track and a gentle walk down the track to Chapman's Peak Drive (30 minutes).

Links: Constantiaberg and Silvermine Nature Reserve (west) via the SABC tarred road; Blackburn Ravine (3.4) via the high contour path from the manganese mine or the lower forestry gravel road.

Difficult terrain: None.

Note: If you wish to visit the manganese mine workings, which are on private land, permission should be obtained from Mr E. Trautmann, Aan de Waterkant, Military Road, Hout Bay 7800. Tel 790-2220.

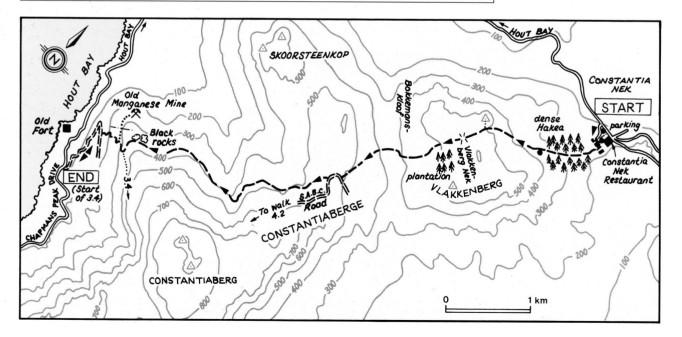

After a rather unattractive start, this route becomes an easy and rewarding walk with particularly fine views of Hout Bay from the western flank of Constantiaberg. Apart from some slopes directly above Constantia Nek which are badly infested with alien plants, the path traverses rich areas of fynbos which are attractive at any time of the year. The route described here is one way; there is public transport from Hout Bay if a car is not waiting for you at the other end. If you consider returning by the same route to Constantia Nek, be prepared for a long day's hike.

The start of this walk is very well signposted. Park at Constantia Nek under the pines and follow the Hout Bay road from a sign reading 'Path to Vlakkenberg' at the Nek.

The characteristic granular appearance of the dark brown rock which was mined above Hout Bay for its manganese content.

Some 100 m down the road a second sign reading 'Pedestrian Access to Vlakkenberg Hiking Trail' points up a small tarred road into a fenced area left – around an underground reservoir – to a gate in the fence, where there is a third sign. Follow a track under blue gum trees past some cottages to the first of a series of small signs with a hiker motif onto a stepped path which leads up past blue gum, *Acacia longifolia* and Black wattle trees into a dense thicket of hakeas. A path has been hacked through this growth, which crowds out the sky. Eventually you will come to an old notice at a fence which marks the boundary between the private land on which you have been walking and the nature area administered by the Regional Services Council of the Cape.

The contrast in vegetation cover is startling and is an object lesson in the devastation that uncontrolled alien plant infestation can cause. On the lower side of the fence there is no sign of plants other than the ecologically barren monotony of a single species; on the other, the beauty of the diverse plants that constitute the fynbos. Those who object to the eradication of alien species from the natural areas of the Peninsula should walk this part of the route and understand why their elimination is necessary.

From the fence, the path climbs steadily to Vlakkenberg Nek, which is reached 50 minutes after leaving Constantia Nek. The bulk of Constantiaberg comes in to view as you drop down from the nek to the stream which flows into Bokkemanskloof west of a corner of the Vlakkenberg plantation. Across the stream the path rises up the northern slopes of Constantiaberg to meet, briefly, the SABC tarred road to the FM tower on the summit. It takes 65 minutes to walk from Vlakkenberg Nek to the tarred road.

Turn right and follow the road for a distance of 50 m or so. Two low poles mark the spot where you leave the tarred road as it swings left (east): take the path which traverses the western slopes of Constantiaberg and drops steadily to the abandoned manganese mine above Hout Bay. From this path there are fine views of Hout Bay, the Sentinel and Karbonkelberg. One spring day – in amongst the charred remains of protea bushes – aristeas and gladiolus were flowering, as were other bulbs stimulated by a recent fire. As I rounded a rock on the path, my reflexes put me into

LEFT: *The ruins of the Old Fort above Chapman's Peak Drive, now a Historical Monument.*
RIGHT: *On the northern slopes of Constantiaberg, beyond Vlakkenberg Nek, the path provides distant views of the southern Hottentots Holland mountains across False Bay.*

rapid reverse even before my mind had consciously identified the shape and colour I had seen on the path as being a Cape cobra. When I cautiously poked my head around the rock – behind a walking stick and an expectant camera – the snake had gone.

Piles of dark brown (some black) rocks of a rough granular texture on a small promontory above Hout Bay mark the top of the workings of the manganese mine (3.4). The manganese is quite distinct from the Table Mountain sandstone in which it is an inclusion (something which occurs sporadically on the Peninsula and in the south-western Cape mountains). From the tarred road to this point takes 50 minutes of steady walking, excluding any reverse travel. Jose Burman surmises that this path was originally used by the Indian labour for the mine.

From the ore piles, the path drops through a series of rather badly eroded zigzags past the turn-off to the manganese mine workings (3.4) to the forestry gravel road. The soil type on this stretch is a shaley conglomerate, orange-brown in colour, and good camouflage for the second snake I saw on the same day: a Puff-adder sunning itself in the middle of the track. At first reluctant to move at my approach, it slithered up the slope after a minute or two, curled itself into a tight spiral under a rock and stuck its head into the centre of this spiral, clearly more afraid of me than I of it. Unless deliberately provoked, snakes on the Peninsula are very seldom aggressive.

It takes 30 minutes to drop down from the manganese ore piles to the junction of the Forestry road with Chapman's Peak Drive 200 m beyond the old forts. If you have not left a car here, a bus to Constantia Nek can be caught in Hout Bay. The fortifications, the well-preserved remains of which are next to Chapman's Peak Drive, are a national monument. They were built by the Dutch East India Company under French supervision between 1781 and 1784. A blockhouse was added by British forces in 1796.

The western slopes of Constantiaberg provide magnificent views of Hout Bay all the way to the manganese mine.

3.2 KARBONKELBERG

An ascent of Karbonkelberg, with a detour to Suther Peak

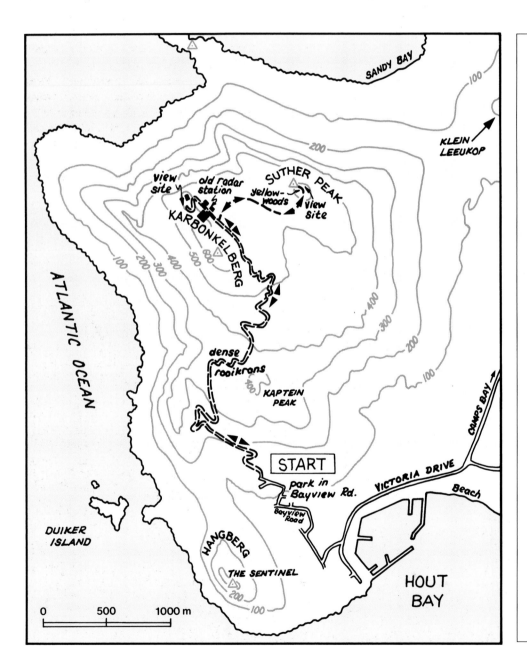

Time: 3 hours.

Height climbed: 450 m.

Exertion: Light.

Start: At the beginning of the track up Karbonkelberg at the top end of Bayview Road in Hout Bay Extension No 15, above the harbour.

Route summary:
1. A steady, gentle climb up the track from the end of Bayview Road, Hout Bay, leading past the ruined radio station to the view site in Karbonkelberg (80 minutes).
2. A short walk back to the junction of the track and the path to Suther Peak (5 minutes).
3. A walk down from the track to a flat area and up a moderate slope on an overgrown path to the ridge on Suther Peak, and back (50 minutes).
4. An easy stroll down the track back to the start (50 minutes).

Difficult terrain: None.

Karbonkelberg is the highest point of the massif which forms the western arm of the mountains surrounding Hout Bay; its southern and western flanks drop steeply into the sea. The sheer northern cliffs of Suther Peak, which is separated from Karbonkelberg by a small flat nek, overlook Sandy Bay and Little Lion's Head above Llandudno. The Sentinel, at the southern end of this land mass, is lower than these peaks, but is a well-known silhouette on the other side of Hout Bay, with vertical sea-facing cliffs above Duiker Island. The whole is separated from the Twelve Apostles by Suikerbossie Nek. Clearly visible is the belt of driftsand driven by millenia of south-easterly winds up the eastern flank of the mountains and over the nek between Little Lion's Head and Suther Peak. This movement of marine sands up the slopes explains why some plants which are normally found growing in dune vegetation at low elevations near the sea are also found fairly high up on the eastern slopes of Karbonkelberg. Prominent amongst these are the tall bushes of *Leucadendron coniferum* which are encountered on the walk up Karbonkelberg: This leucadendron grows only in wind-blown calcareous sand. Another striking example of this anomalous vegetation is provided by the orchids, *Satyrium carneum*, which flower along the track in the same area in November. These are robust plants, with flowering stems up to a metre high topped with a dense cluster of pink or pink-and-white flowers, your first sight of which will stop you in your tracks. *Satyrium carneum* grows elsewhere on the dunes.

The other vegetation on these mountains is characteristic of the substratum – shale on the lower slopes, with outcrops of granite on the western seaboard topped with Table Mountain sandstone. There is one plant, however, which has an interesting history. *Serruria collina*, a member of the Proteaceae family and related to the Blushing bride (*Serruria florida*), was first recorded by the famous plant collector

Arum lilies, Zantedeschia aethiopica, *flower amongst the restios on the damp flats between Karbonkelberg and Suther Peak.*

James Niven at the end of the 19th century, but he was characteristically vague and described its locality as 'Table Mountain'. Only a few years ago, Prof W.P.U. Jackson, author of *Wild Flowers of Table Mountain*, and Dr J.P. Rourke, Curator of the Compton Herbarium at Kirstenbosch, discovered its locality when they chanced on a population of these plants on the steep south-facing slopes of Karbonkelberg. I was recently lucky to come across another population near Suther Peak. It is now evident that these plants are closely related to (or are probably the same

species as) plants found on the hills around Glencairn (also very rare) and known as *Serruria flagellaris*.

Another somewhat unusual aspect of the vegetation here is the appearance of trees such as Yellowwoods (*Podocarpus latifolius*) and Cape coast cabbage trees (*Cussonia thyrsiflora*) in amongst the rocks on the open, higher eastern slopes, together with Camphor bushes (*Tarchonanthus camphoratus*). Although these are low-growing (a muted echo of the forests in Orange Kloof not far away), they are an indication that before man started burning the veld and felling the

trees, the forests on the Peninsula were not just confined to kloofs and the eastern side of Table Mountain.

The route up Karbonkelberg scarcely needs description. To get to the start of the walk, drive along the harbour road in Hout Bay past Mariner's Wharf. Just before the factory area, turn into an unnamed road to the right which shortly meets Karbonkel Road at a T-junction; turn right, then right again into Bayview Road and follow this road all the way up the slope to its end, which is the start of the track up Karbonkelberg. The Karbonkelberg area is now man-

LEFT: *Chapman's Peak and Noordhoek Beach appear over the nek between the Sentinel and Karbonkelberg as you climb.*

ABOVE: Protea scolymocephala *grows on the sandy area half-way up the eastern slopes of Karbonkelberg.*

aged by the Nature Conservation Department of the Cape Provincial Administration and entry to the public is permitted, despite the old signs at the start of the track and further along at a gate, now permanently open. The track winds up the slope, runs along a damp, steep shale slope

From the top of the ridge on Suther Peak, Lion's Head appears beyond the last of the Twelve Apostles and the slopes of Little Lion's Head.

then zigzags through a small kloof to emerge onto a sandy area where *Leucadendron coniferum* and *Satyrium carneum* are first encountered. This area is badly infested – in places overgrown – with alien *Acacia cyclops*, and for a distance the track is enclosed by dense walls of it. Higher up, the track zigzags through the rocks, and one encounters the beginnings of forest described above. The first signs of a former military presence are piles of rubble from demolished buildings next to the track. As the track levels out to the north of the beacon on Karbonkelberg, the first of the abandoned buildings which once were part of a radio station comes into view. Some 50 m before the first of these, note a small path leading off to the right (north) which is marked by a low cairn of stones: this is the path to Suther Peak. The track continues past the first building, then doubles back and back again to a small nek where a few steps to the left brings you to a spectacular view of the boiling sea below and the distant Chapman's Peak, Noordhoek Beach and Kommetjie. The track peters out just beyond this point. The views from are spectacular. It takes about an hour and a half to reach this point from the start.

The detour to Suther Peak is well worth a little extra effort. It takes five minutes to walk from the viewpoint on Karbonkelberg to the start of the path to Suther Peak. This path is overgrown in places, particularly on the slope of Suther Peak, but always clear. The path first drops down to a flat area, which it crosses, heading in a north-east direction, before climbing fairly steeply up to the rocks on Suther Peak. Ignore a branch to the right as the path starts to rise. Just before the path attains the top of the ridge, it passes through a delightful patch of Yellowwood forest and at the top it emerges from the trees. From the rocks on top of the ridge, there is an impressive view of Sandy Bay, almost directly below, and of Little Lion's Head, a near perfect imitation of its larger namesake up the coast. The northern cliffs of Suther Peak are sheer and their descent is not recommended. The walk to Suther Peak and back to the track takes 50 minutes. Another 50 minutes brings you back to the start of the track up Karbonkelberg.

Karbonkelberg has a rich and interesting vegetation and the walk up its slopes provides some spectacular scenery.

TOP RIGHT: *An orb-web spider* (Argiope sp.) *spins its web between low bushes in the fynbos.* BELOW RIGHT: *The butterfly,* Danaus chrysippus, *on* Scabiosa africana.

ORCHIDS

In the Cape Peninsula there are 100 species of orchids, all of which have 'protected' status in terms of a Government Ordinance. All are terrestrial and some are amongst the most spectacular flowering plants to be seen here. The Pride of Table Mountain, *Disa uniflora*, is so well known that it is the emblem of the Mountain Club of South Africa and the Western Province Rugby Union. Nevertheless, the sight of Red disas flowering in summer (January and February) on a stream side or in a damp rock crevice is unforgettable. Red disas can be seen in a number of places on Table Mountain, including Fir Tree Stream near Maclear's Beacon, Echo Valley, Window Stream, Skeleton Gorge, the top of Disa Gorge and De Villiers Reservoir.

Equally beautiful are the pale mauve flowers of the Blue drip disa, *Disa longicornu*, which grows on damp rock ledges and flowers slightly earlier (December and January). The Blue disa, *Herschelia graminifolia*, is found growing on sandy slopes, flowering in autumn in amongst low restios, generally high up on the mountain. Perhaps the largest orchid on the Peninsula is *Satyrium carneum*, whose flowering stems, up to a metre high, carry a spike of tightly packed pink flowers in late spring. It is generally to be found growing in sand dunes or sandy coastal areas but also occurs fairly high up on Karbonkelberg. Many orchids are seldom seen except after a fire. *Pterygodium catholicum*, a small yellow-flowered orchid, is one of these.

Orchids have highly specialised flower parts which allow pollination only by specific insects. Red disas are pollinated exclusively by a large butterfly, the Table Mountain beauty (*Meneris tulbaghia*).

Pterygodium acutifolium *flowering in a recently burnt patch of fynbos atop Fernwood Buttress.*

Herschelia graminifolia, *the Blue disa, has scented flowers and grows on open mountain slopes.*

Disa longicornu, *the Blue drip disa, is confined to damp seepage areas on rock faces.*

Satyrium carneum, *the largest orchid on the Cape Peninsula, can grow to 1 metre high.*

Disa uniflora, *the Red disa or Pride of Table Mountain, on a stream bank.*

Monadenia densiflora, *is stimulated to flower by fire.*

3.3 CHAPMAN'S PEAK

An ascent of Chapman's Peak from Chapman's Peak Drive and a traverse on the contour path between Chapman's Nek and Blackburn Ravine

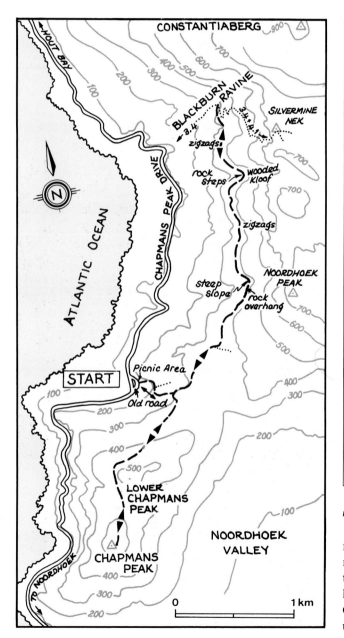

Time: From the parking area to Chapman's Peak takes 1 hour and 20 minutes and the return 50 minutes. From Chapman's Nek to Blackburn Ravine takes 55 minutes and the return 45-50 minutes.

Height climbed: 450 m to Chapman's Peak; 550 m to Blackburn Ravine.

Exertion: Moderate.

Start: The parking area (a loop of the old road) on Chapman's Peak Drive 4,8 km from the turn-off to the beach from the Main Road in Hout Bay.

Route summary:
1. A moderate climb from Chapman's Peak Drive to Chapman's Nek (20 minutes).
2. From Chapman's Nek an easy walk up a gentle gradient past Lower Chapman's Peak to Chapman's Peak (1 hour).
3, An easy stroll from the peak back to the nek (35 minutes).
4. A traverse from Chapman's Nek to Blackburn Ravine on a path which climbs and drops somewhat but is generally on the contour (55 minutes), and back (40-45 minutes).
5. A moderate climb from Chapman's Nek back down to the start (15 minutes).

Options: The walk along the contour path to Blackburn Ravine from Chapman's Nek is optional.

Links: Silvermine Nek (3.4) and the abandoned manganese mine above Hout Bay (3.4).

Difficult terrain: Next to the contour path there are some steep slopes, but the path is easy and safe along its entire length.

The sheer cliffs of Chapman's Peak, which drop almost vertically into the sea, have impressed innumerable motorists on Chapman's Peak Drive, one of the most scenic roads on the Peninsula. The walk up Chapman's Peak from this road is easy and even more rewarding. Although not as high as Noordhoek Peak and Constantiaberg to the north, Chapman's Peak is far enough from other peaks to be a unique vantage point with grand views in all directions.

The path up Chapman's Peak runs on the western side of Lower Chapman's Peak before the final climb to the top.

The walk from Chapman's Nek in the opposite direction on the contour path which runs along the western faces of Noordhoek Peak and the Silvermine mountains to Blackburn Ravine is also described here, as it is a logical extension of the Chapman's Peak walk, which can be linked to the paths from Blackburn Ravine to Hout Bay and from Blackburn Ravine to Silvermine Nek.

The name Chapman for the peak and the bay enclosed by Noordhoek Beach was given by the captain of a British ship, the *Consort*, which arrived in the bay on 29 July 1607. John Chapman, the mate of the vessel, was sent to look for a suitable anchorage and both the bay and the peak were named after him.

There is an established parking area with concrete tables and chairs for picnickers (on a loop of the old road off Chapman's Peak Drive) at the foot of the valley which leads up to Chapman's Nek. The path starts up the left-hand side of the stream on some rock steps, then, a short way up the

valley, it crosses the stream. Ignore a path which heads straight up alongside the stream; instead, walk for a few metres on one of the two short paths south until you get to a path coming from the right. Turn left up this path, which climbs straight to Chapman's Nek on an eroded path covered with loose stones (these can be trying when coming down). On the nek – a sandy area with low restioid growth in a fire-break, reached after 20 minutes – you will come to a crossroads. To the left, over some low rocks, is

the beginning of the contour path to Blackburn Ravine; straight on is a minor path up the slope of Noordhoek Peak. The Chapman's Peak path is to the right. At the edge of the firebreak it enters a dense stand of *Protea lepidocarpoden-*

BELOW LEFT: *South of the beacon on Chapman's Peak, the long stretch of Noordhoek Beach leads to Slangkop Lighthouse.*
BELOW: *The contour path between Chapman's Nek and Blackburn Ravine passes a forested ravine flanked by vertical cliffs.*

dron, which is characteristic of the shaley soil over which the path runs as it rounds the western side of Lower Chapman's Peak. As the path climbs steadily towards the small nek between Lower Chapman's Peak and Chapman's Peak itself, there is a changing view of Hout Bay, Karbonkelberg and the Sentinel. The proteas are interspersed with Kreupelhout (*Leucospermum conocarpodendron*) from whose yellow pincushions Orangebreasted Sunbird males challenge others and chat to their mates. In the nek, densely packed *Leucadendron xanthoconus* bushes mark the transition to Table Mountain sandstone. The path climbs through this growth from the nek to the jumbled rocks which mark the top of Chapman's Peak and on which the beacon stands. It takes one hour to walk from Chapman's Nek to the peak.

From the beacon there are distant views all round. The FM tower on Constantiaberg looms over Blackburn Ravine to the north past the Silvermine mountains; to the east lie the Fish Hoek/Noordhoek Valley and False Bay; to the south, the white sands of Noordhoek Beach lead to Slangkop lighthouse; to the west, a remote Karbonkelberg crouches over Hout Bay. You can sit here like a Greek god on Olympus and watch the waves break white on the rocks almost vertically below, while toy cars crawl along a miniaturized Chapman's Peak Drive. Black lizards bask on the rocks around you, and butterflies sample the flowers. Far away across the bay, launches take visitors to view the seals on Duiker Island below the Sentinel.

The walk back from Chapman's Peak to Chapman's Nek takes just 35 minutes. From the Nek it is only a 15-minute walk back to the parking area, but if you wish to extend the route or link up with the paths from Hout Bay or Silver-

mine, take the contour path north – it is simply an extension of the path from the peak.

The contour path climbs gently from the nek on the slopes of Noordhoek Peak and crosses a small stream before climbing onto clay soil which is typical of these slopes all the way to Blackburn Ravine. Further along, the path passes a rock overhang with yellow Lachenalias flowering in the damp shade, and drops down to cross a stream bed in a small kloof. On the other side, the path is wide and safe but there is a steep fall away from it. The path continues on the contour, then drops down a zigzag and crosses another stream bed. Beyond this, a drip-face on vertical rock is the home of yellow spiloxenes, purple-blue geissorizas and ixias which vie with the *Selago* on the slope below to produce the most delicate shades of blue and lavender. The path enters a wooded kloof, more beautiful than

FAR LEFT: Pterygodium catholicum, *an orchid found in sandy areas.*
CENTRE: *From Chapman's Nek, the mountains of the Silvermine Nature Reserve and Kalk Bay rise over the Noordhoek valley.*
ABOVE: Erica cerinthoides *is well adapted to fire: after a burn, the stems sprout rapidly from the underground root stock and the plant can flower within a year.*

Blackburn Ravine, out of which it climbs over several rock steps to continue on the contour, with a steep fall away on the left. Round a buttress and past a vertical rock face, it drops down again through a zigzag into the last small kloof before Blackburn Ravine. Walk down some rock steps and round a buttress, and the trees in Blackburn Ravine come into view. It takes 50-55 minutes to walk from Chapman's Nek to the cement weir in Blackburn Ravine. The return route, surprisingly, takes less – 40-45 minutes.

3.4 BLACKBURN RAVINE

A walk from Chapman's Peak Drive to Blackburn Ravine, an ascent to Silvermine Nek and down again and back via the high contour path to the manganese mine

Time: 3½ hours, including one hour to Silvermine Nek and back, and 10 minutes to the manganese mine and back.

Height climbed: 350 m to the high contour path; 550 m to Silvermine Nek.

Exertion: Moderate to high.

Start: At the beginning of the gravel track on Chapman's Peak Drive, 1,6 km from the turn-off to the beach from the main road in Hout Bay.

Route summary:
1. An easy walk from Chapman's Peak Drive to the weir in Blackburn Ravine (50 minutes).
2. A steep zigzag climb from the weir, first on the west, then on the east side of the stream, to the junction with the high contour path (25 minutes).
3. A very steep zigzag climb from the high contour path junction to Silvermine Nek (30 minutes) and back (30 minutes).
4. A level, then gently dropping, traverse of the south slope of Constantia-

berg on the high contour path from Blackburn Ravine to the junction with the path from Constantia Nek on an overgrown path (45 minutes).
5. A short zigzag descent to the forestry track (with a 10-minute detour to the manganese mine if desired) and a gentle stroll down the track to the start (20-25 minutes).

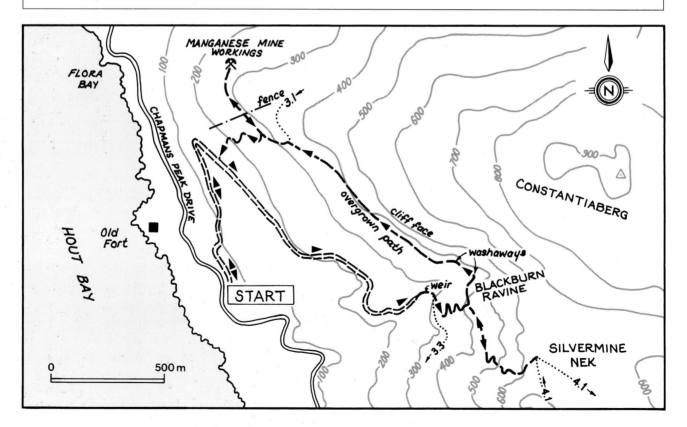

Options: The climb from the start of the high contour path to Silvermine Nek is optional. A visit to the manganese mine is optional.

Links: The Chapman's Peak contour path (3.3); Silvermine Nature Reserve via the nek (4.1, 4.2); Constantia Nek from the manganese mine (3.1).

Difficult terrain: The climb up to Silvermine Nek is on a steep slope which in places drops away almost vertically from the path for a short distance; the path is wide and safe, however. There is a short scramble up some rocks shortly after you leave the ravine on this path. The first part of the contour path from the ravine to the manganese mine is on a steep slope but with no exposure; this path is in disrepair with minor washaways in two spots.

Note: The manganese mine is on private land. Permission to visit the mine should be obtained from Mr E. Trautmann, Aan de Waterkant, Military Road, Hout Bay 7800; Tel 790-2220.

Silvermine Nek is directly above Blackburn Ravine and provides a unique vantage point for views to the west of Hout Bay and, to the east, of False Bay.

A Bobartia species in bud, with its characteristic restio-like leaves, grows next to the high contour path from Blackburn Ravine.

Blackburn Ravine, on the steep south-western slopes of Constantiaberg, is the meeting place of four paths – the path (initially a forestry track) from Chapman's Peak Drive; the contour path to Chapman's Peak; the path up a steep slope just to the south of the ravine to the nek in the Silvermine Nature Reserve; and the path which leads from high up the ravine on the contour under the cliffs to meet the path from Constantia Nek. This walk includes three of these; the climb to the nek overlooking the Silvermine Nature Reserve is included because it provides a link with walks in the reserve and because it is only an hour's detour off the otherwise circular route.

The walk starts on the gravel forestry track on Chapman's Peak Drive, 1,6 km from the turn-off to the beach from the main road in Hout Bay and just past the entrance to the forester's house. There is parking space here.

The track at first runs up the slope away from Blackburn Ravine before doubling back to head towards it. It then becomes a path which winds around the slopes into the ravine, where for a short while it runs next to the forest before meeting the stream under the trees. Here there is a small cement weir built over an older brick structure which is now supplemented with a plastic pipe to provide water

for the small pipeline to the now defunct Forestry Station, the original reason for the path. It is a gentle 50-minute walk from Chapman's Peak Drive to the weir.

Across the stream is the start of the contour path to Chapman's Peak Nek and Chapman's Peak itself. Don't cross the stream, however, but take the path which leads up sharp left (west) of the stream from the weir. This zigzags up the slope for a short stretch, then leads up the stream over the rocks for 20 m or so before crossing to the east side and emerging from the trees. A cairn of rocks marks the crossing point. This is the start of a series of zigzags up the steep slope including, at one spot, a scramble up some rocks. This ends at a right-hand turn where the path heads south-east, rising gently towards a rock-face. Mark this turn, because it is the junction with the high contour path (the route to take on the return from Silvermine Nek) which is, in fact, just a continuation at this point of the path from the nek. This point is reached after 25 minutes' climbing from the weir.

The path to the nek turns away from the rock-face and zigzags all the way up a very steep slope, emerging at a broad nek with Constantiaberg on the left and a rocky slope on the right. The slope to the nek faces Hout Bay and there are increasingly impressive views of the bay, Karbonkelberg and the Sentinel as you climb until, at the nek, these mountains are dwarfed. The path up the slope is obvious at all times and although in places it drops very steeply from the path, nowhere is there any danger. It takes only 30 minutes to climb from the junction with the high contour path to the nek and about the same to return to this point. The diversion is well worthwhile for the views of Hout Bay and on the nek itself east to False Bay and the Hottentots Holland Mountains. Return from Silvermine Nek to the junction of the high contour path and the path up from the cement weir in Blackburn Ravine.

The high contour path leads back into Blackburn Ravine, crossing it above the forest and leading west directly under the vertical cliffs. The slope below the path is steep, but there is no exposure as the path crosses minor washaways in two streams and runs next to a little waterfall. These south-facing cliff faces are permanently damp. On the seepage areas grows a wide variety of flowers which are a delight in spring and early summer. The slopes below the cliffs are covered with proteoid fynbos and the path runs through thick stands of proteas. In places along the path where the proteas have overgrown the path, it is a bit of a struggle to break through. The path is always easy to follow, however, as it is marked with stone cairns at intervals. It drops gently, heading west all the time and leaving the cliffs, until eventually it meets the path from the western side of Constantiaberg and Constantia Nek (3.1) as it zigzags down the slope to the forestry track. It takes 45 minutes to walk from the junction with the Silvermine Nek path to the junction with the Constantia Nek path.

Here, take the well-worn path leading down in the direction of Hout Bay – it swings sharply left in a zigzag. Before the end of this zigzag there is a clear path to the right, and a five-minute walk along this track past the fence which marks the boundary of private land brings you to piles of dark stones. This is manganese ore, the remains of opencast mining of a seam of ore which took place at the turn of the century. The first pile of ore is on a platform built of rock. This was used as a base to shovel the ore into a chute which took it down the mountainside to be loaded aboard ships down below. The mining operation ceased after a few years as it was uneconomic. Beyond the platform are other ore-piles and a deep gouge in the mountain as evidence of further mining activities.

The walk down the mountain follows the zigzag path to its junction with the forestry track. Here you turn right and follow the track back to the start; this takes 20 minutes.

Chapman's Peak dominates the bay below Chapman's Peak Drive. Kreupelhout bushes are prominent on these slopes.

CHAPTER 4

SILVERMINE

FAR LEFT: *The reservoir surrounded by pines in the Silvermine Nature Reserve (west).*
LEFT: Gladiolus debilis, *one of the Painted ladies, flowers in the mountains in spring.*

The Silvermine Nature Reserve, administered by the Cape Town City Council, occupies an area which effectively forms a belt across the midriff of the Peninsula. It is bisected by the Ou Kaapse Weg, which climbs its northern slopes, passes the entrances to the western and eastern sides of the reserve and then runs along the valley which separates these portions, eventually dropping into the Fish Hoek/Noordhoek Valley, which forms the southern boundary of the reserve. Constantiaberg (not part of the nature reserve) is situated at its north-west corner, and the western boundary is formed by the escarpment – which includes Noordhoek Peak – overlooking Hout Bay. On the eastern side of the reserve is a series of peaks – Muizenberg Peak, Kalk Bay Mountain, Ridge Peak and Cave Peak – which overlook False Bay. There are two pine plantations on either side of the Ou Kaapse Weg. Apart from these alien plantings, the reserve is covered with rich and diverse natural fynbos. In the valleys between Kalk Bay Mountain, Ridge Peak and Cave Peak small patches of Afromontane forest are found.

It is strange that the name Silvermine has persisted, because there never was a silver mine here, simply because there never was any silver. Although the Here XVII, who constituted what would now be called the board of the Dutch East India Company, had a test shaft dug to check for the presence of any precious metals at a site now marked by a sign on the side of the Ou Kaapse Weg, only traces of manganese were found, and no mining took place.

A unique feature of the peaks above Kalk Bay is their caves. Some of these have been known a long time, but most were only discovered and explored in the course of this century. T.V. Bulpin tells the delightful story of a J.B. Meyer, a school teacher who retired in ill-health to Kalk Bay in 1935. While on holiday eleven years before, Meyer had become fascinated by the caves in these mountains and had even discovered two new caves. In his retirement, he gathered round him a group of fellow enthusiasts who called themselves the Moles, Meyer being the First Mole, and over the years, this group discovered many more caves in the area. Meyer eventually died in 1952 aged 78; his diary recorded 1 700 climbs into these mountains over a period of 19 years – a long lease of life for a man who retired early due to poor health!

While there is no guarantee that walking in this area will prolong your life, it will certainly enrich it. In this chapter are described five walks – two in the western side of the Silvermine Nature Reserve, including the popular Panorama Circuit and Constantiaberg walks, and three in the eastern side – which cover most of the reserve and its features. Silvermine Nek (3.4) provides the link between walks on the western side of the reserve and the routes above Hout Bay.

4.1 PANORAMA CIRCUIT

A walk to Noordhoek Peak, a traverse of the western peaks above Hout Bay to Silvermine Nek and a return over the plateau

Time: 2¾-3 hours.

Exertion: Moderate.

Height climbed: 500 m.

Start: The parking area in the Silvermine Nature Reserve (west) near the reservoir.

Route summary:
1. From the parking area, a steady, gentle climb on a path and finally a track to the viewsite above Noordhoek Valley (50-55 minutes).
2. From the viewsite, a gentle climb, first on a gravel track, then on a sandy path, to Noordhoek Peak (15 minutes).
3. From Noordhoek Peak, a strenuous route which leads steeply up and down the rocky slopes of the peaks between Noordhoek Peak and Silvermine Nek (50-55 minutes).

4. A gentle stroll back to the parking area from Silvermine Nek along a track which drops down in zigzags with a moderate gradient to the valley floor (50-55 minutes).

Links: Constantiaberg (4.2); Blackburn Ravine (3.4); Chapman's Nek (3.3).

Difficult terrain: On the traverse from Noordhoek Peak to Silvermine Nek there are two minor rock scrambles up the first of two steep slopes. On the way up the next peak, the path ascends very steeply next to a vertical cliff; one point on this section is very exposed. To avoid this scramble up the slope to the right through the bushes and back to the path at the top of the peak. This section of the path may be re-routed shortly.

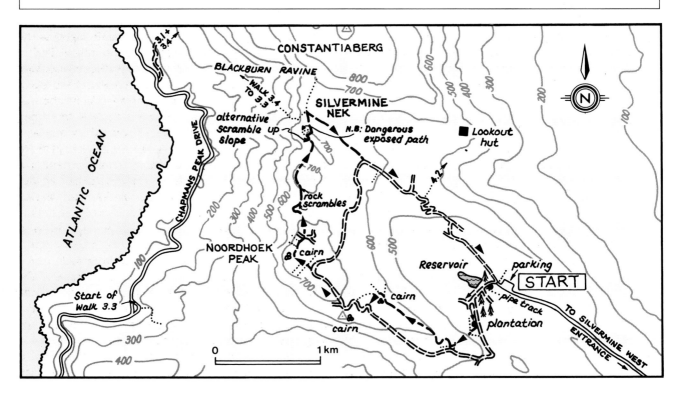

Watsonia tabularis, *named after Table Mountain, flower on the sandy flats of Silvermine Nature Reserve (west). False Bay is in view beyond* the Muizenberg and Kalk Bay Mountains.

This route is aptly named, as this is one of the most scenic walks in the Peninsula with wide and distant views from almost every point. Noordhoek Peak and the unnamed peaks between it and Silvermine Nek which drop very steeply to the west to Hout Bay are (as seen from the Bay) really just rocky outcrops on the edge of the plateau. Despite the grandeur of the scenery, this is not a difficult or strenuous route – with one important exception (*see* Difficult Terrain page 134) which can be very easily and conveniently avoided.

To reach the start of the walk, drive up the Ou Kaapse Weg to where a clearly signposted tarred road leads right (west) off the top to the gate of the Silvermine Nature Reserve where a small entrance fee is charged. Continue along the narrow tarred road to the parking area which terminates it. From the western end of the parking area, start walking on the gravel road which leads over the stream (to your right pines partly obscure the concrete wall of the reservoir). Just across the stream a path starts on the left, signposted 'Pipe Track'. Continue on the gravel road to a point adjacent to the southern end of the reservoir wall. Turn left on the road, which leads uphill with a pine

plantation on your left (ignore a road to the right) to the start of a path on the right signposted 'Noordhoek Peak'.

Take this path, which winds up a small valley overlooking the reservoir through fynbos dominated by bushes of Kreupelhout (*Leucospermum conocarpodendron*). Along the way you step over a rock quite different from the surrounding grey Table Mountain sandstone rocks and the white sand derived from them; this is igneous rock with veins of white quartz running through it, evidence of some ancient geological upheaval. The path heads towards a small nek, but branches before reaching this nek. The left-hand branch leads over the rise to join the gravel road, which has taken a wider loop to reach this point. Ignore the left-hand branch and continue on the right-hand branch, which swings right and then runs next to sandstone rocks which have weathered to show their stratified structure perfectly. The path continues up and down some rocks on the reservoir (north) side of the ridge, then passes a boulder and climbs steeply to its left, eventually climbing to the ridge itself. From here, to the east, False Bay – bounded in the distance by the southern Hottentots Holland Mountains – is spread out behind you. Constantiaberg, crowned

135

Beyond Constantiaberg are glimpsed Fernwood Buttress on Table Mountain and Devil's Peak; Leucadendron xanthoconus bushes colour the veld on the ridge above Silvermine Reservoir.

by the apparently not quite vertical FM tower, rises above the plateau to the north, with Fernwood Buttress on Table Mountain and Devil's Peak in view behind.

On the ridge, the path comes to a crossroads marked with a small cairn. To the right is a minor path to a lookout point. Straight on is a path which winds round the slopes above the plateau and below the gravel road, eventually meeting this road before it drops down the zigzags into the valley where the reservoir is situated. Take the path left, which drops to meet the gravel road; there is a minor path which branches right off this path near the cairn to meet the gravel road higher up. Turn right on the gravel road which swings south up the slope to a beacon on the left. The beacon and a large stone cairn nearby are on the edge of a steep slope down to Noordhoek Valley. Dominating the scene is the white sweep of the sands of Noordhoek Beach with Slangkop lighthouse at its farther end. The near end of the beach is obscured by Chapman's Peak and Lower Chapman's Peak. From the parking area to the beacon is a walk of 50-55 minutes.

From the beacon, walk back to the gravel road. At this point the road turns through a right-angle and heads north. Ignore a sandy track which leads west off the turn to become a small path which drops down the slope to

stone cairns to guide you over the rocks, eventually rounding the head of one of the very steep kloofs above Chapman's Peak Drive. From here the path heads straight up the steep slope of the next peak. There are two minor rock scrambles on the way, but these provide no problems. From the top the path winds down the other side through the rocks to the head of the next kloof. Parts of this section of the route are not obvious, but a reliable succession of stone cairns marks the way. At the bottom of the slope, with the kloof falling away to the left, the path heads straight up the steep slope of the next peak, emerging from some rocks halfway up the slope to turn left on the contour directly towards a cliff. Here the path climbs up a very steep slope just next to the near-vertical rock face and one part on this section of the path is dangerously exposed with an unprotected drop to the left. It is not necessary to use this steep section of the path, however, as it is very simple to climb from the foot of this section up the fairly steep slope to the right, avoiding all rocks, to meet the path on the top. Anyone doing this route in reverse should note that the degree of exposure on this section of the path is not evident from the top. Turn right on the path which drops steeply down through the rocks to Silvermine Nek with the rounded bulk of Constantiaberg rising on the other side. It takes 65-70 minutes to walk from the beacon overlooking Noordhoek peak to Silvermine Nek. This is a fairly new route; the old Panorama route simply followed the gravel road, from which the rugged scenery along the newer route is hidden. The steep, short section of the path which encompasses the dangerous exposure may soon be rerouted up the neighbouring slope.

On Silvermine Nek there is deep sand in great danger of erosion after fire. The track which leads east from the nek has anti-erosion logs across it at intervals. This track shortly joins the gravel road where the latter swings east, and passes another dressed-stone signboard lacking its sign which marks the end of the lower path from the ridge leading to Noordhoek Peak. The gravel road then drops through some zigzags into the valley surrounding the reservoir. At the bottom, at an intersection, take the road right, and shortly after (at a second intersection) the road left, which leads to the parking area. This section of the route is the least spectacular, but if you raise your eyes from the admittedly rather slippery road (the result of loose gravel), False Bay floats like a mirage before you along the way. This last section of the route is a gentle stroll of 50-55 minutes.

Chapman's Nek. Instead, continue on the gravel road north up a rise to the start of a sandy path which branches left at a dressed-stone signpost which lacks its sign. Take the path which comes to a crossroads after a few metres. The right-hand path joins the gravel road again; the main path leads straight on, but it is worth a two-minute detour on the left-hand path to a large stone cairn which marks the top of Noordhoek Peak. At the cairn, the whole of Hout Bay lies at your feet; turn round, and all of False Bay is spread before you.

Return to the main path and turn left (north) along it. The path crosses a track before climbing up through the rocks of an outcrop, down again and up the rocky slope of a minor peaklet to swing steeply down right with little

4.2 CONSTANTIABERG

An ascent of Constantiaberg from the Silvermine Nature Reserve (west), visiting Elephant's Eye Cave and returning via Silvermine Nek

Time: 3¼ hours, including the side trip to Elephant's Eye Cave and the walk across the summit to the western beacon.

Exertion: Moderate.

Height climbed: 450 m.

Start: The parking area in the Silvermine Nature Reserve (west).

Route summary:
1. From the parking area in Silvermine (west), a walk with easy gradients up to the lookout hut (40 minutes).
2. A walk with some easy rock scrambling up to Elephant's Eye Cave (10 minutes) and back (10 minutes).
3. A climb from the lookout hut, fairly steep in places, to the top of Constantiaberg (50 minutes).

4. A walk from the top of Constantiaberg down to Silvermine Nek (35 minutes).
5. An easy stroll from the nek down to the start (45 minutes).

Links: The Panorama circuit in Silvermine (4.1); Constantia Nek and the manganese mine, Hout Bay (3.1), via the SABC tarred road or Silvermine Nek (3.4).

Difficult terrain: None.

With a height of 927 m Constantiaberg is the second-highest independent mountain on the Peninsula after Table Mountain. Climbing it, however, is comparatively easy, with none of the puffing and panting associated with most of the routes up Table Mountain. This is essentially a circular route (aside from the initial stretch) which leads up Constantiaberg past Elephant's Eye Cave and down the southern slopes to Silvermine Nek.

To reach the start of this walk, drive over the Ou Kaapse Weg and turn off to the Silvermine Nature Reserve (west) on the tarred road marked 'Reservoir'. There is a charge per person and per vehicle to enter the reserve. Continue along the tarred road through the reserve to the signposted parking area and park there.

Start walking on the gravel road which leads due west from the parking area next to a pine plantation up the valley. At a junction, turn right and, at a second junction,

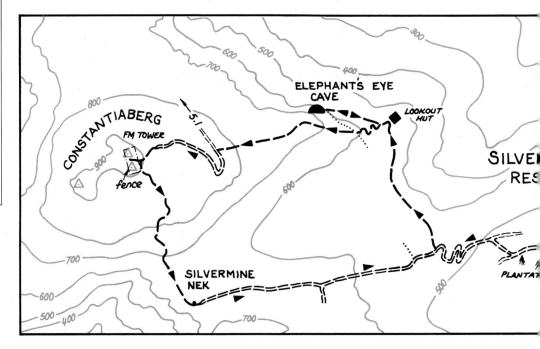

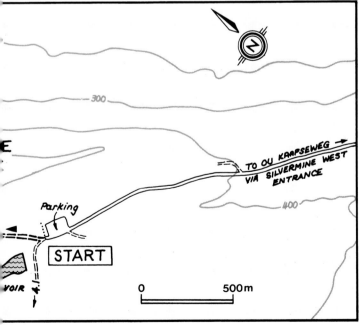

Agapanthus africanus flower on the steep slopes of Constantiaberg *above Silvermine Nek. Chapman's Peak almost hides Noordhoek beach in the distance.*

left. The road zigzags up the head of the valley and continues west over a rise. Before the road breasts the rise, a well-trodden path leads off to the right, where the road continues due west across the flats. Take this path, which drops down over some rocks next to a plantation of pines to a stream and rises on the other side on the slope of Constantiaberg. One summer's day I disturbed a large brown bird perched on the rocks above the plantation. I was unable to identify it, as it flew to the top of a nearby pine, but later it joined three others circling lazily above Prinskasteel Stream. These I immediately recognised as Black Eagles, so the bird I first saw must have been a juvenile. The sight of four of these great raptors soaring effortlessly in the sky was magnificent. A forestry lookout hut is visible at the end of a low ridge. Up the slope the path branches at a small sign depicting an elephant. Take

the right-hand branch which leads to the top of the ridge next to the lookout.

Elephant's Eye Cave is clearly visible from this point and is reached in 10 minutes along a path marked with another sign depicting an elephant. The path to the cave is rather stony and involves some easy scrambling up rocks. What is not evident from the ridge is how large the cave is. It is a strange shape, uncharacteristic of the Table Mountain sandstone from which it was hollowed by a process which is not obvious; most caves in this type of rock are really overhangs. Legend has it that this was once the refuge of a princess, leader of a Khoi-Khoi tribe; its old name was Prinseskasteel, but this name, now corrupted to Prinskasteel, has been given to the stream running south of the cave. Return to the ridge the same way.

The path up Constantiaberg starts up the ridge and across the steep, wet south slope in a series of zigzags. Ignore the shortcuts on this stretch, which cause erosion, as well as two poorly defined paths to the right to Elephant's Eye Cave along the first part. At one spot, the slope drops away steeply from the path, but it is quite safe. The path rises to a small nek with good views south over the Silvermine Reserve and continues up the slope to meet the tarred SABC road to the FM tower on the peak. Turn left on the road and follow it all the way to the transmission tower and associated buildings.

A high fence immediately surrounds the FM installation, and a dilapidated low old fence encloses a larger area around this. There is an unfortunate amount of rubbish strewn around here, including the dangerous remains of broken fluorescent light tubes; the SABC would do the public a favour by cleaning all this up.

There are three beacons on Constantiaberg, the two easterly close to each other and the FM tower. The beacon to the west is reached in 10 minutes by a poorly defined path over the rocks from the other beacons. At one point, a bit of rock scrambling is required to cross a gully. From all three beacons the views are grand. The top of Constantiaberg is very rocky, a dramatic foreground for a wide vista of Table Mountain, Orange Kloof, Grootkop, Hout Bay and the rest of the Peninsula to the south.

For the return journey, follow the fence around the FM tower to its south-west corner, just below the southernmost beacon. From this corner, walk about 25 m along the southern fence where a path branches to the right past a very obvious cairn of stones. Take this path, which is small but always clear and well marked along the way with stone

LEFT: *The Red crassula,* Crassula coccinea, *and* Selago serrata *colour the summer fynbos veld on the eastern slopes of Constantiaberg.*
ABOVE: Erica hirtiflora, *aptly named for its hairy flowers, grows in dense fynbos on seepage slopes or alongside streams.*

cairns. The path drops increasingly steeply down the slope, with Hout Bay harbour coming into view. Just before it drops onto Silvermine Nek the path passes a stone cairn on the shale band which is characteristic of the sea-facing slopes on this side of Hout Bay. The nek itself is very sandy and in danger of serious erosion.

Logs have been laid along the first sandy portion of the path which leads from the nek eastwards to join a gravel track. Continue on the gravel track across the flats to the zigzags which lead to the valley surrounding the reservoir. At the first road junction at the bottom of the zigzags turn right and shortly after left on the gravel track which runs past the pines along the reservoir back to the parking area.

4.3 STEENBERG

An ascent of Steenberg Peak from the Silvermine Nature Reserve (east) entrance and a return via Junction Pool and the waterfall

Time: 2¼ hours.

Height climbed: 250 m.

Exertion: Light.

Start: The parking area at the gate to the Silvermine Nature Reserve (east).

Route summary:
1. A steady climb from the entrance to Silvermine (east) to the top of Steenberg (40 minutes).
2. An easy downhill stroll from Steenberg past Junction Pool to the waterfall, with a 10-minute detour to the fall then back to the start (90 minutes).

Links: Muizenberg circuit (4.4); St James circuit (4.5).

Difficult terrain: None.

Looking out over (and almost a mere stone's throw away from) one of the busiest roads on the Peninsula – the Ou Kaapse Weg – Steenberg supports a rich and unspoilt fynbos flora with a good complement of birds, animals and insects. From the peak, which is really just the highest point of an escarpment, you can gaze out over Cape Town's southern suburbs while around you swallows roller-coaster down the wind and Painted ladies (*Gladiolus debilis*) nod to each other. Here the threshold from a man-made environment to a natural one is easily crossed. This is one of my favourite short walks, as you can find yourself in totally natural surroundings within 15 minutes of setting out.

To reach the start of this walk, drive over the Ou Kaapse

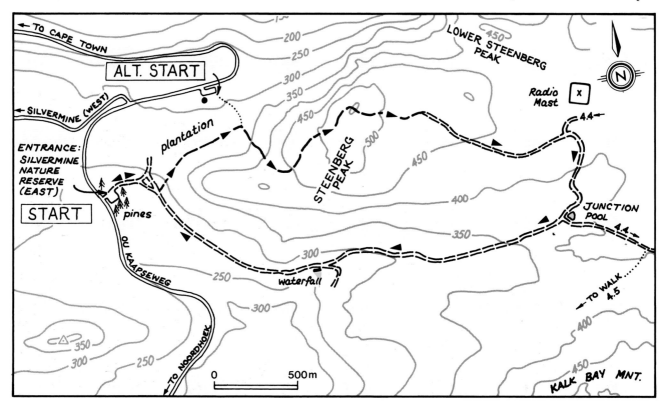

TOP RIGHT: *A large stand of* Erica urna-viridis *grows on the eastern slopes of Steenberg. The plants have a rather straggly habit, but the sticky flowers are uniquely beautiful.* BELOW: *A typical patch of fynbos on the lower south-eastern slopes of Steenberg with Noordhoek beach just visible in the distance.*

Weg from Cape Town past the entrance to the western part of the Silvermine Nature Reserve to the entrance to the eastern side; this is easy to overshoot, as you come up to it suddenly, but it is marked by tall pines growing next to it. At weekends you can take a car further into the pine plantation, but there is little point, so rather park under the pines at the entrance.

Take the track past the gatehouse into the pines; where this emerges on the southern side of the plantation, turn left next to the plantation and walk over the rise on its boundary to its south-east corner. This point can also be reached from a limited parking area on the Ou Kaapse Weg just as it clears the rise and heads west to the Silvermine

(west) entrance; parking here is not always available but, if you do park here, just walk up next to the plantation to its south-east corner.

The path leaves the plantation corner and heads west across a stream in a firebreak. Don't take the first path right, which is badly eroded, but continue to the correct path which turns right up the valley over a series of stone steps. This is the only steepish part of the walk and it is short. The path swings left to the head of the little valley. Shortly after passing between two large rocks, the path appears to split. Do not continue straight on; this is not a proper path but the beginnings of an erosion channel. Turn sharp left on an obvious path up the slope. This crosses a small flat sandy area before climbing slightly and winding up to Steenberg Peak, not quite on the edge of the mountain. It is worth, in fact, taking one or two of the small paths left off the main path to get an uninterrupted view of the southern suburbs and eastern side of Table Mountain. From

the peak itself, which is not very obvious, there are views east to the Hottentots Holland Mountains on the other side of False Bay. Next to the path there is a large overhang, not really a cave, which can provide shelter if necessary. It takes 40 minutes to reach Steenberg Peak from the gate at the entrance to the reserve.

This section of the walk is dominated by some large, old bushes of Kreupelhout (*Leucospermum conocarpodendron*) and *Mimetes fimbriifolius* which, because of their thick, corky bark, can survive fires. They are therefore very old, and when they flower in spring, they provide a magnificent sight. This is a rich fynbos area and amongst the many beautiful plants are Painted ladies (*Gladiolus debilis*) which flower at the end of September. The top of Steenberg has some amazingly shaped rocks, carved by the wind and the rain. On the north-facing ledges are a few isolated plants of the rare endemic *Erica halicababa* wedged into crevices in the rocks.

From the peak the path drops down to the east through a large population of a beautiful erica species, *Erica urna-viridis* to a flat sandy area where it meets a track. There are paths and shortcuts all over the flats but it is easiest to stick to the track. Ignore a branch left off the track which leads to a SADF prohibited area behind a wire fence. Follow the track as it swings round the lower slopes of Steenberg to the west to Junction Pool, the meeting place with the track leading south which joins up with paths from St James (4.5) and Muizenberg (4.4). Junction Pool is a pleasant place to stop. The track continues next to the stream, which is not visible, overgrown as it is with Keurbooms and other vegetation. The Keurboom, a magnificent sight in flower in October, is a forest pioneer, an indicator that the streamside vegetation is a potential natural forest in the making. Shortly after the track meets another track from the left, there is a short but steep path off to the left to the waterfall. This is, in all honesty, no Victoria Falls, but it is worth a

LEFT: *The Silvermine Nature Reserve is the ideal place for a walk in winter. Flowering bushes of* Leucadendron laureolum *seem to glow against a stormy sky over Constantiaberg.*

ABOVE: *The spectacular everlasting* Edmondia sesamoides *flowers in early summer on the flats between the top of Peck's Valley and Steenberg before the path swings down to Junction Pool.*

visit. More interesting than the waterfall itself are the trees in the kloof below. It is only a five-minute scramble to the waterfall down a path which is signposted. From the waterfall, the gravel track swings round the mountain, rising slightly through denser fynbos, lit up in winter with the brilliant yellow colours of *Leucadendron laureolum*, before reaching the plantation, then the way back to the gate and start of the walk. From the top of Steenberg it is a gentle 90-minute walk back to the start.

4.4 Muizenberg Peak

An ascent of Muizenberg Peak from Boyes Drive by way of Peck's Valley, returning down Mimetes Valley

Time: 2¾ hours.

Exertion: Moderate.

Height climbed: 400 m.

Start: At the beginning of the path up Peck's Valley, a portico in a stone wall next to a 'Silvermine Nature Reserve' sign above Muizenberg on Boyes Drive, 3,9 km from its start off the Main Road to Muizenberg.

Route summary:
1. From Boyes Drive, a steady, easy climb up Peck's Valley to the junction with the Muizenberg Peak path (50 minutes).
2. A moderate climb to Muizenberg Peak (15 minutes) and back (10 minutes).
3. A gentle stroll from the radio masts down to Junction Pool (20 minutes).
4. After a short, easy uphill walk, a detour to Muizenberg Cave (15 minutes there and back), followed by an easy stroll down Mimetes Valley to a point where the path drops down very steeply

on zigzags to Boyes Drive (50 minutes).

Links: Spes Bona Valley (4.5) via the path over Kalk Bay Mountain or the track to Oukraal; Steenberg (4.3).

Difficult terrain: None.

Muizenberg Peak stands at the north-eastern corner of the Silvermine Nature Reserve above the town of Muizenberg. Its northern and eastern slopes above Boyes Drive are steep, with almost vertical cliffs directly below its summit. This allows uninterrupted views of the whole of the eastern flank of Table Mountain, the southern suburbs of Cape Town, the Cape Flats and False Bay.

To get to the start of the route, turn off the Main Road to Muizenberg onto Boyes Drive which traverses first the northern, then eastern lower slopes of Muizenberg Peak. Some 3,9 km from the turn-off, on the mountain side of

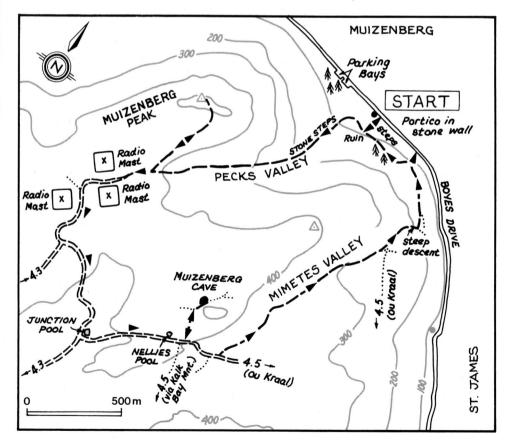

146

TOP RIGHT: *Restios growing alongside the track past Junction Pool.*
BELOW RIGHT: *Muizenberg Peak drops sheer to the east, revealing a spectacular view of Muizenberg, False Bay and the southern Hotten-tots Holland mountains.*

Boyes Drive, there is a stone wall, halfway along which is an opening next to a 'Silvermine Nature Reserve' sign. There is limited parking in some bays under some Stone pines just before the wall: these are in front of private properties – please do not trespass onto them. A sign points along Boyes Drive to the start of the Peck's Valley path, and through the wall, stone steps lead up to a row of Stone pines flanking a ruined stone building where the steps meet a path at a T-junction. The path up Peck's Valley is the right-hand (north) branch, which contours round into the valley and climbs steadily on a well-made path of stone steps up the left-hand slope. Above the slope to the right in the rock face of Muizenberg Peak there is a huge over-hang with trees at its mouth.

As the path gains the higher reaches of the valley, it becomes steeper. Near the top of the valley it crosses the stream bed to the right-hand slope and becomes sandy. Here, in the natural surrounding of low fynbos, dotted with white and cream everlasting flowers in summer, a mosaic of ericas and restios with brilliant splashes of colour from the purple *Pelargonium cucullatum*, an utterly incongruous sight appears: the top of one of the SADF communications masts sticking out of the head of the valley like the top of a crane on an industrial building site. This is one of three masts, each surrounded by a fenced-off area, which occupy the flats between the head of Peck's Valley and the eastern slopes of Steenberg. All three are an eyesore, yet vital to the functioning of the maritime communications centre on the slopes of Steenberg below. Before the path reaches the fences, it becomes a sandy track for a few metres and here a small but well-defined path leads at an angle back to the right, up Muizenberg Peak. Peck's Valley is named after two brothers, Simon and Henry Peck, who ran Farmer Peck's Inn which stood at the foot of the valley early last century. The walk from Boyes Drive to the masts takes 50 minutes.

The beacon on Muizenberg Peak can be reached easily in 15 minutes and the detour is well worth the small effort. Ten minutes sees you down by the radio masts again.

Take the track which leads between the two fences towards the fence surrounding the third mast where it swings first left (ignore the track to the right), then right next to the fence before turning left to meet the gravel track up the eastern slope of Steenberg. Turn left onto the gravel track which follows the course of a stream surrounded by a dense growth of fynbos typical of a moist habitat. In the valley, the track comes to a grove of Keurboom trees which have been planted next to Junction Pool, a small cement weir. It is only a 20-minute walk from the top of Peck's Valley to Junction Pool. Here marked by a low nature reserve sign, a track leads left off the gravel track up a low rise in a valley the sides of which are covered with bushes of *Mimetes fimbriifolius* and Kreupelhout. Over the rise there is the small man-made pool, Nellie's Pool, on the left; as you approach the pool, you may be startled by the splash of the frogs taking to the water. Some 40 m down the track past Nellie's Pool, a clear small path to Muizenberg Cave leaves the track on the left. It is a six-minute walk up through the rocks to the cave mouth. The cave itself is large with some dark passages leading off it, and a back entrance. On the path to the cave, you pass some massive old bushes of *Mimetes fimbriifolius*, one very ancient patriarch, suitably bearded with lichen, looking as if it has collapsed under its own weight. It is still alive, however. This species, endemic to the Peninsula, shares with the Kreupelhout (*Leucospermum conocarpodendron*), a degree of fire resistance provided by thick corky bark. Even after a fire which will burn off their leaves and young branches as well as the surrounding vegetation, these species can resprout from growth points under the bark. A lot of these Mimetes bushes in this area have survived countless fires and have become very old

With False Bay in the background, Pelargonium cucullatum *flower at the top of Pecks' Valley.*

indeed. Mimetes Valley, the route down to Boyes Drive, is aptly named, although its lower reaches could just as well be called 'Pincushion Valley' from the dense stand of Kreupelhout there.

A short distance down the slope beyond the start of the path to Muizenberg Cave, the gravel track meets another gravel road at a sharp angle from the right. (Some 200 m up this track you will find the start of the path up onto Kalk Bay Mountain.) The combined gravel tracks swing round the eastern slopes of Kalk Bay Mountain to Oukraal, just beyond the start of the path up Spes Bona Valley.

Take the path down Mimetes Valley which leads left off the junction of the two tracks past a fence which denies vehicles access to a parallel sandy track which ends shortly. As is fit, the slopes are dominated by large *Mimetes* bushes as the path descends. Along the path are plants of *Protea* *speciosa*, one of the most beautiful proteas, with pink bracts tipped with brown fur. The species has adopted another strategy to cope with fire. Like the King protea (*Protea cynaroides*), it has a ligno-tuber from which it can send up new shoots after a fire has burnt off all its stems above ground. *Protea speciosa*, which rarely occurs in great numbers in any one locality, is an indicator of reasonably well-watered areas. The sandy path is eroded in places and heads straight towards Seal Island in False Bay. The southern Hottentots Holland Mountains seem to hover before you as you descend. Lower down, the path descends more and more steeply down stepped rocks to the top of a steep slope at the bottom of which you can see the thatched roof of Bailey's Cottage between the railway line and the sea. From this point the path heads left along the slope to a very steep, stepped descent and meets a path which runs along

The lower reaches of Mimetes Valley drop steeply, providing a vertiginous view of Bailey's Cottage below.

the flat top of a rock on the contour. Take the left-hand path, which leads down a rather eroded section of path and shortly comes to a branch. To the right, a short series of cemented stone steps drops directly down to Boyes Drive. To the left, the path climbs a bit to meet the stone steps from the start of the Peck's Valley path at the ruined walls under the Stone pines. Either way can be used to reach Boyes Drive and the start of the route. From Junction Pool to the start is a 50-minute walk.

LEFT: *Table Mountain and the suburbs of Cape Town are visible below the steep slopes of Muizenberg Peak.* BELOW: Cryptadenia gran-diflora *grows on flat, sandy areas.* BOTTOM: *A beacon marks a subsidiary peak on Muizenberg beyond which Cape Point is just visible.*

LICHENS

Exposed Table Mountain sandstone rocks would present a rather uniform, dull appearance were it not for the growth of lichens on them. These growths provide a fascinating variety of colours and patterns which transform the appearance of their substrate. Not all lichens grow on rocks; old tree trunks and branches, like those illustrated, often carry Old Man's Beard (*Usnia* spp) or other lichens.

There are three broad categories of lichens: crustose lichens are thin and lie flat on the surface of their substrate, often in a more or less circular pattern; foliose lichens produce leaf-like growths from their point of attachment; and frucitose lichens look like small, many-branched plants.

Lichens are not single organisms. They are the outward form of an intimate and symbiotic relationship between a photosynthesising alga and a fungus. Experiments have shown that the individual organisms can grow perfectly well by themselves, even in contact with the other organism, when there is no shortage of nutrients. Lichens are formed when nutrition is limiting. The fungus wraps itself around the cells of the alga and even penetrates them to tap the products of photosynthesis; in this condition the alga cannot reproduce. Sometimes the outward appearance of the symbiont is that of the fungus but often a new form is produced. It is these which provide the range of colours and patterns which make them so decorative.

Lichens have been (and still are) used as the source of a range of natural dyes for handmade textiles, including the famous Harris tweeds of Scotland.

Because they absorb nutrients efficiently from dust and drops of moisture in the atmosphere, they are sensitive to industrial pollution – in Lapland reindeer were seriously contaminated after feeding off lichens which had absorbed radiation resulting from the Chernobyl nuclear disaster in the USSR.

A frucitose lichen clothes the bark of a very ancient Mimetes fimbriifolius *tree near Muizenberg Cave.*

4.5 THE AMPHITHEATRE

A walk up Echo Valley to the Amphitheatre, returning via Spes Bona Valley

Time: 2¾-3 hours, including the detour to Cave Peak.

Exertion: Light.

Height climbed: 400 m.

Start: Above St James, on Boyes Drive.

Route summary:
1. From Boyes Drive, a steady, gentle climb up to Oukraal (20-25 minutes).
2. A gently sloping walk up Echo Valley through the Amazon Forest to the Amphitheatre (1 hour) with a detour to Cave Peak (15 minutes).
3. A short, fairly steep climb out of the Amphitheatre and over the ridge on Ridge Peak; thereafter an easy stroll down Spes Bona Valley back to Oukraal with one very easy rock scramble in the forest (50 minutes).
4. A stroll back down the Mule Track to the start (20 minutes).

Links: There are several paths linking this route with the Muizenberg circuit (4.4) and the Steenberg circuit (4.3).

RIGHT: *Shrubs of* Leucadendron strobilinum, *a member of the Protea family, line the path above the Amazon forest in Echo Valley between Ridge Peak and Cave Peak. From here there is a magnificent view over False Bay towards Hangklip. Further along, several paths lead off to some of the numerous caves which are found in this area.*

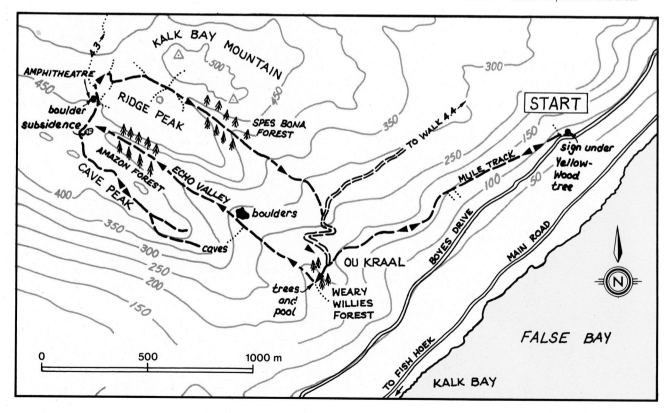

The Amphitheatre is a small, sandy depression surrounded by rocky slopes in which there are several caves, one of which – Blue Disa Cave – is named after the Blue drip disa (*Disa longicornu*) which grows on the damp rock ledges at its entrance and flowers in early summer. In Echo Valley there is a small patch of forest, optimistically or jokingly called the 'Amazon'. Although small in extent it is, nevertheless, lovely, as is a similar but larger patch in the adjoining Spes Bona Valley.

Both are classic examples of the Afromontane forests which characteristically occupy well-watered kloofs of the south-western Cape mountains. In the Spes Bona forest there is a large population of *Haemanthus coccineus* (April fool flowers); their pairs of broad, strap-shaped leaves (lying flat on the ground) carpet the forest floor. This population of plants never flowers, but reproduces vegetatively. Clearly the spot where they grow was, some time in the past, not covered by trees. The 'natural' extent of Afromontane forest in the south-western Cape has been much debated. What is clear is that it is not constant but fluctuates in response to medium-term changes in climate and the severity and frequency of fires, as well as the season during which they occur.

To reach the start of the walk by car, turn off the Main Road to Muizenberg into Boyes Drive. Some 5,1 km along Boyes Drive, at the apex of a sharp left-hand curve, there is a Silvermine Nature Reserve signboard under a Yellow-wood tree. Park off the road beyond the curve. Ignore the stone steps leading up to the right and start walking on the Mule Track which heads left (southwards) gently up the slope. Some 20-25 minutes of steady climbing, with views of St James, Kalk Bay Harbour and Simon's Town below, brings you to Oukraal. Here a gravel track meets the Mule Track from the north, a small path from Boyes Drive meets it on the left and the path itself drops down the slope ahead on stone steps to the stream below, passing on the left another path down to Boyes Drive. At the stream, there is a well-used picnic spot under the trees (a small forest in the making), known as Weary Willie's.

Just across the stream, take the path which heads straight up the valley by means of some stone steps and ignore any side paths. You pass a group of large boulders on the right, a shady place to stop. The path then crosses to the right-hand side of the valley before entering the Amazon Forest. Here there is a shaded clearing (a delightful resting place) from which the path continues on the right-hand side of the stream bed for a few metres before crossing the stream

and rising along its left bank under the trees. It takes only five minutes to walk the length of the forest. As the path emerges from the forest, Cape coast cabbage tree (*Cussonia thyrsiflora*) bushes grow alongside blister bushes. You cross the stream again where stone steps lead up to a fork in the path. Here, between the two arms, the ground has subsided, evidence of the continuing formation of caves in these mountains. The left-hand path leads up onto Cave Peak, a worthwhile 15-minute detour for the views into Fish Hoek Valley and to Kommetjie, and for access to the caves. The mountains in this area are well known for their many caves. Some of them are dangerous, so do not try any impromptu caving. For more information on the caves, contact Mr L.W. Hall, Secretary of the South African Speleological Society in Cape Town, Tel 21-2430 or 75-6480.

From this path another path leads west down into Klein-tuin Kloof to join a track which links up with a gravel road which is part of the Steenberg circuit (4.3). From the branch, stone steps lead up right past a minor path to the right into the Amphitheatre. This is a pleasant place to stop and explore. It takes one hour to climb up Echo Valley from Weary Willie's to the Amphitheatre.

The Amphitheatre is criss-crossed with minor paths, but the exit route leaves via a large rounded boulder on the south-west side of the Amphitheatre; the path starts at the boulder's northern side and goes straight up the slope over

BELOW: *The Mule Track from Boyes Drive to Weary Willie's at the bottom of Echo Valley provides splendid views of the coast on the eastern Peninsula.* LEFT: *A female Orangebreasted Sunbird.*

rocks and through bushes and low Yellowwood trees. Although the path is a bit overgrown, it is clear. Once the bush has been left behind, the path branches. The left-hand branch continues to rise to a small nek and then drops to join the gravel road leading to Kleintuin Kloof. Take the right-hand branch, which climbs steeply up onto the ridge of Ridge Peak and, passing a minor path to the left, swings east along the ridge, passing a minor path back into the Amphitheatre on the right. At another branch, take the right-hand path which heads east to Spes Bona Valley. At the top of the valley the path branches again. A well-defined path to the left climbs steeply up stone steps on to Kalk Bay Mountain. Take the right-hand path, which is badly eroded in deep sand and leads into the valley. Very shortly, the path enters the Spes Bona Forest.

On a hot, sunny day, the contrast is delightful: outside, the light is white and intense, while under the trees it is subdued and soft. The going is gentle, generations of fallen leaves cushioning your steps. At one spot, where there is a scramble down some rocks (with a fallen branch to help you down), the Yellowwoods frame the vertical cliff alongside and patches of moss on it glow golden-green in the sun. As you walk through the forest, dropping steadily all the time, the muffled sound of the sea increases steadily, then suddenly as you emerge from the trees and see False Bay directly ahead. A steep, stony section of the path leads straight down and joins a gravel track; turn right (south) here. The track zigzags down the slope and shortly meets the top of the Mule Track. The walk from the Amphitheatre onto Ridge Peak and down Spes Bona Valley to the Mule Track takes 50 minutes. The start is reached after a gentle 20-minute stroll back down the Mule Track with the breakers off Muizenberg Beach echoing the curve of False Bay always in view.

LEFT: *Cave Peak looms over False Bay and the distant Hottentots Holland.*

CHAPTER 5

CAPE OF GOOD HOPE NATURE RESERVE

FAR LEFT: *The new Cape Point lighthouse situated far down on the rocky promontory is visible even when low cloud covers the top of the ridge.* LEFT: *A pair of African Black Oystercatchers.*

When the Portuguese explorer Bartholomeu Dias rounded Cape Point in 1488, he knew he was the first European to have reached the southern end of the African continent. Not that Cape Point is the southernmost tip of Africa, but from this point the coast stretches in an easterly direction. The significance of this event is huge, as the establishment of the trade route around the Cape provided the material basis for the flowering of European civilisation which was to transform the world in succeeding centuries.

Dias named the point the Cape of Storms, but it was renamed *Cabo de Boa Esperanza* (Cape of Good Hope) by the King of Portugal. This name is now given to the twin peak which marks the southern tip of the Peninsula, and 'Cape Point' to the rocky promontory to its east and slightly north of it. Compared with Table Mountain these are tiny peaks, but they mark the southern limit of an area which is every bit as beautiful scenically and is as rich in flora and fauna, namely the Cape of Good Hope Nature Reserve, commonly called Cape Point.

Cape Point occupies some 7 750 ha at the southern tip of the Peninsula. There is always an argument about where the Atlantic and Indian oceans meet, but there is no doubt that at Cape Point the cold waters of the Benguela current of the West Coast meet the warmer waters of False Bay, which are fed by the Agulhas current of the East Coast. Overlooking False Bay is a low range of mountains with Judas Peak and Paulsberg prominent; the eastern cliffs of

these peaks fall almost vertically to the sea. To the west the range slopes more gently down to the plains which cover most of the reserve and extend to the west coast, where in places there is a small rocky escarpment above the shore. Most of the reserve is covered with highly leached, acid sands derived from Table Mountain sandstone. At Bordjiesrif on the east coast, however, are some low limestone hills formed by the accretion of the remains of ancient marine organisms and, also near here, plumes of calcareous drift sand of more recent origin blown up onto the land by the strong south-easterly winds. On the Rooihoogte, a low ridge near the entrance, are slopes covered with shale-derived soil. Below the Table Mountain sandstone rocks of Cape Point and the Cape of Good Hope lies a bed of granite which resists the pounding of the waves; these would have washed away the historic cliffs aeons ago if the granite had been absent. Large areas of the plains are seasonally water-logged; in general, wetlands form one of the most threatened types of ecosystem in the south-western Cape and the conservation of the reserve's areas is important. A unique feature of the reserve is Sirkelsvlei (*see page 165*), a small perennial lake on a high part of the plateau without any apparent water supply; the water level is, in fact, maintained by seepage, except in times of exceptional drought.

The wind is perhaps the most dominant weather factor in the reserve. Domineering would perhaps be a better description for some of the south-easterly gales that roar in summer and the north-westerlies in winter. The wind and the poor, thin soils in the reserve ensured that farming was never practicable. Despite this, after the British occupation of the Cape and the establishment of the Simon's Town naval base, farms in this area were allocated to a few brave souls. John Osmond, formerly a ship's carpenter, was granted the first farm – Buffelsfontein – and later bought Uiterstehoek, which included Cape Point. The present Homestead Restaurant incorporates John Osmond's original farmhouse. The farmers must have lived hard, impoverished and isolated lives. One successful venture, however, was the production of lime from the limestone.

It is due to the far-sightedness and determination of a few individuals that South Africa has conserved some of its natural areas. The Cape of Good Hope Nature Reserve is no exception. After World War I there were plans to develop holiday resorts along its coast. Fortunately Dr S.H. Skaife, an entomologist and keen naturalist, together with R.H. Compton, a previous Director of the National Botanic Gardens at Kirstenbosch, and others, continued to campaign for the establishment of the reserve. In contrast with its present active promotion of conservation, the then Cape Town City Council scornfully rejected the idea, but after sufficient funds were collected by public subscription, the Divisional Council of the Cape (now the Western Cape Regional Services Council) bought Smith's Farm, which incorporated the land originally owned by John Osmond,

Helichrysum vestitum stands out in the Cape Point fynbos in the face of an approaching north-westerly storm.

midshipman on HMS *Bacchante*, noted in his diary, 'At 4 am the Flying Dutchman crossed our bows'; his observation was confirmed by the lookout and officer of the watch. There is nothing insubstantial, however, about the many wrecks along the shore of the reserve.

The management of the reserve includes the preservation of its fauna and flora, particularly rare and endangered species; the eradication of all alien species; anti-erosion measures; and scientific research.

Recently, with the advent of the idea that functioning ecosystems should be preserved, the conservation emphasis in the reserve is changing. In line with many other conserved areas, 'Nature Reserve' tended to be interpreted as 'Game Reserve', with the emphasis on the preservation of the larger and more obvious mammals. At Cape Point, heroic efforts were previously made to keep blue and black wildebeeste herds, but these antelope were never recorded from the area, the plant cover of which is quite unsuited to these animals. It is certain that the bontebok, the most visible buck in the reserve, were in fact here before; eland and red hartebeeste were recorded from the area but were probably migratory, a behaviour no longer possible. Certainly, the favourite browsing of the eland is the invasive alien acacias, not the fynbos, and the bontebok favour grassy areas regenerated after fire. In attempts to provide grazing for these animals, many parts of the reserve have been frequently burnt to the detriment of the vegetation, a practice of the previous farmers in the area. The Regional Services Council has now accepted that the reserve is primarily a botanical reserve, and management practices, in particular the policy of frequent block burns, will be modified accordingly. Buck which were known to be permanent residents of the area such as grey duiker, steenbok, vaal rhebok, klipspringer and grysbok will be conserved, as will the small mountain zebra herd.

The Cape of Good Hope Nature Reserve offers many forms of recreation to its more than 400 000 visitors each year. For the walker (still a rarity here), it is a visual feast. There can be few other places in the world offering such a combination of varied scenery, colour and natural and historical interest.

The management of the reserve is, at the time of writing, expanding its nature trails. The three walks described in this chapter are an introduction to the delights of this area.

and the Cape of Good Hope Nature Reserve was eventually proclaimed in 1939, with Norman Smith its first warden. Since that time neighbouring farms have been bought to bring the reserve to its present extent. Dr Skaife is remembered in the name of the research centre at Olifantsbaai.

From the time shipping from Europe began to round the Cape five centuries ago, Cape Point was notorious for its dangers. The turmoil at the meeting place of two major ocean currents, the high winds and submerged rocks and reefs combine to make conditions treacherous for ships. Hendrick van der Decken and the crew of a 17th-century Dutch ship were lost without trace while attempting to round the Cape against strong headwinds. The ghost of this vessel has reputedly been sighted by many, including King George V of Great Britain, who on 11 July 1881, as a

5.1 SIRKELSVLEI

A walk from Olifantsbosbaai to the wreck of the Thomas T. Tucker and Sirkelsvlei

Time: 2¾-3 hours.

Exertion: Low.

Height climbed: 100 m.

Start: The parking area at Olifantsbosbaai in the Cape of Good Hope Nature Reserve.

Route summary:
1. An easy walk from Olifantsbosbaai, along the coast and past the wrecks to the fence at Brightwater (40-45 minutes).
2. A gentle climb to the start of the new Sirkelsvlei path on the escarpment (30 minutes).
3. A level walk across the flats to Sirkelsvlei (35 minutes).
4. A level walk from Sirkelsvlei back to the coast, across the flats and then along the flank of the valley, finally dropping steeply down to Olifantsbosbaai (1 hour).

Option: There is a direct route from the Olifantsbosbaai parking area to the start of the new trail to Sirkelsvlei (25 minutes).

Difficult terrain: None.

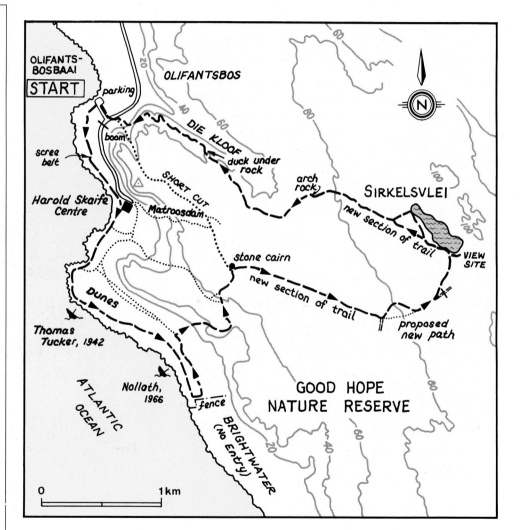

This walk has everything – except altitude! Pristine coastal and montane fynbos, birds, buck, beach and a shipwreck are all included but, above all, this route provides a feast of scenery, especially in spring when the colours of the leucadendrons, restios, ericas and a host of other plants combine to provide a sight which matches the splendour of Namaqualand at this time of year but in a more subdued and subtle way.

The weather here is as wild as the scenery. In winter, north-west gales batter the coast and in summer a strong south-easter is common. Some of this walk is over areas which in winter can be very wet.

The route starts at the Olifantsbosbaai parking area. To get here from the entrance of the Cape of Good Hope Nature Reserve, take the well-signposted turn-off right to Olifantsbos about a kilometre from the entrance. This road leads directly west for a kilometre or two to a T-junction. Take the road to the left which leads directly to the parking area. Keep to the general speed limit of 40 km/h in the reserve (although you are likely to find that most of the vehicles of visitors and the Nature Reserve staff will pass you at anything up to twice this speed) because then you will get a chance to spot the buck and birds. Bontebok are usually to be seen near Olifantsbosbaai.

The walk starts on the south-west side of the parking area between the low blue gum poles where a way has been cleared through the bush adjoining the coast. At first a

RIGHT: *The wreck of the* Thomas T. Tucker *which was carrying a cargo of tanks when it ran aground during World War II.* BELOW: *Brightly coloured lichens colour the rocks near Olifantsbosbaai.*

Sacred Ibis fly down to feed on the rocks next to the beach at Olifantsbosbaai. These birds usually fly in a V-formation.

track, the path leads from the vegetation over some scree, the rocks beautifully marked with lichen, and then follows the high-water mark between the bush and the coastal rocks to the small bay in front of the Harold Skaife Education Centre. This centre is used, amongst other things, as a base by researchers from universities and the National Botanic Institute, Kirstenbosch for their work on the ecology of the fynbos and the coast. Follow the curve of the beach to the rocks at its southern end. On the way, you may disturb a flock of Avocets, looking, against the white sand of the beach, like jumbled notes on the score of some avant-garde composer's music. Beyond the rocks is another small bay. As you round the dunes at the end of this bay, the wreck of the *Thomas T. Tucker* comes suddenly into view. The *Thomas T. Tucker* was an American liberty ship carrying tanks when it ran aground in 1942 while trying to escape the attentions of a German U-boat. It is a walk of 25-30 minutes to the wreck. About half a kilometre along the beach are the less impressive remains of the *Nolloth*, a Dutch coaster wrecked in 1965, beyond which is the first corner of a fence which marks the boundary of an area closed to the public, namely Brightwater; at the end of the beach, the coastline is also fenced off.

At the first fence corner, which is reached about 15 minutes after leaving the wreck of the *Thomas T. Tucker*, take a track which leads back north; five minutes along this track a branch to the right (east) leads up the slope to a nek and over the ridge in mature fynbos before it swings left up the head of a valley to a branch in the track. Take the right-hand branch, which shortly meets a well-worn track at a T-junction. Turn right along the track which swings northwards through some curves on the plateau behind the Harold Skaife Centre. Some 30 minutes' walk from the beach and five from the T-junction, look out for a path to the right (east) marked by a low cairn of stones. This is a newly laid-out trail which heads east, keeping to the high ground to avoid marshy areas.

After a 15-minute walk, the new trail leads over some rocks to a T-junction with a well-worn track. Turn left along the track, which turns through right-angles right then left. Where some branches bar the way on a small rise, another new path has been laid out which leads directly to the eastern end of Sirkelsvlei, a walk of about 20 minutes. Here there is a turn-off to the right to a viewpoint from which a path leads down to the water's edge.

From the viewpoint, the new trail skirts the southern shore of the lake. About 500 m from the viewsite, next to a large rock, a path branches to the right to bring you to the north-western end of Sirkelsvlei where there is a small sandy beach bordered by buffalo grass. From here, the path loops back to the main path which then heads away from the vlei in a westerly direction. The path passes through a natural rock archway and past a rock shaped like the eye of a needle where it changes direction south and crosses over two streams in a shallow valley before turning westwards again, now on the level top of the southern flank of the valley which drops away to the right. Towards the edge of the escarpment, the path passes through the rocks and you have to duck through a short, low passage under a massive boulder. Beyond this there are some rocks on edge, the strata at right angles to the ground. With the parking area of Olifantsbosbaai in view, the path swings left across the bluff and drops into a small valley which debouches onto the entrance to the parking area. It is an hour's walk back to the start from Sirkelsvlei.

Although the total walking time is only some 3 hours, this is really a day walk because there are so many interesting things to explore along the way.

For those interested only in Sirkelsvlei, there is a shorter way to it. The entrance to the parking area at Olifantsbosbaai faces a small valley up which a gravel track runs. This track leads directly to the start of the new walking trail to Sirkelsvlei. From Olifantsbosbaai to this point it is only a 25-minute walk.

Ticks are plentiful; after a walk, ape the baboons!

SIRKELSVLEI

A unique feature of the Cape of Good Hope Nature Reserve is Sirkelsvlei, a small perennial lake on a raised part of the plateau inland from Olifantsbosbaai. It has no apparent water supply; the water level is, in fact, maintained at least partly by seepage from the surrounding areas, except in time of extreme drought. Because this water percolates through acid sands with a high proportion of dead vegetable matter, it carries a high concentration of humic acids which colour the waters of the vlei a deep brown peaty colour. It would be expected that the water in the vlei would also be acidic, like the water in streams and man-made waterholes elsewhere in the reserve. It is, in fact, neutral, which may be evidence of another, subterranean source of water for the vlei.

The water tastes brak but tests have indicated that it is not very saline. It is possible that it is stale, lacking in oxygen because of poor aeration in the vlei and because the seepage supply is also poorly aerated. Although the vlei has some aquatic life – for example, the Cape river frog (*Rana fuscigula*) and freshwater shrimp – it does not attract much bird life. It does, however, provide a watering place for red hartebeest and bontebok during the dry summer months. Not a great deal is yet known about this mysterious body of water but nobody can deny its beauty.

Homoglossum priori *flowers on the north bank of Sirkelsvlei.*

5.2 KANONKOP

A short walk to the signalling canon on Kanonkop and down to the old lime kiln at Bordjiesrif

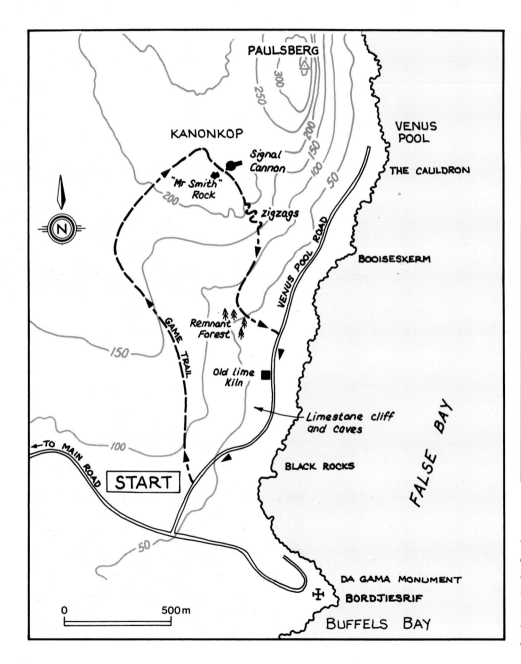

Time: 1 hour 20 minutes.

Exertion: Light.

Height climbed: 200 m.

Start: In the Cape of Good Hope Nature Reserve, 250 m along the tarred road to Venus Pool which turns left off Bordjiesrif Road, 1,2 km after Bordjiesrif Road leaves the main road to Cape Point.

Route summary:
1. A moderate climb from the Venus Pool road to the signalling cannon on Kanonkop (40 minutes).
2. A steep climb down to the lime kiln on the coast followed by a short climb back up to the start (40 minutes).

Difficult terrain: None.

TOP RIGHT: *The signalling cannon on Kanonkop seems to be aimed at the southernmost tip of the Cape Peninsula.*
RIGHT: *The doleful face of Mr Smith, an unusual rock formation just below Kanonkop.*

There has been some dispute about the former function of the old cannon which was found wedged in the rocks on what is now called Kanonkop, but it is now thought most likely that it was the first of a series of signalling cannons used by the Dutch East India Company to warn of the approach of ships. It is well known that what was probably the second signalling cannon in the line was at Simon's Town.

About thirty years ago, Mr Ernest Middlemiss, a previous warden of the reserve, obtained plans from Holland for a gun-carriage for the cannon. He then built such a carriage – it is the one on which the old cannon still rests. As the carriage is more likely to have suited the deck of a ship rather than the rocks at Kanonkop, it is possible that the position in which the cannon was found was, in fact, its historical one.

Although the cannon provides an interesting destination, this short circular walk is also ideal as an introduction to the many natural pleasures that walking in the reserve can provide. This is a new trail and the route may change somewhat in future, so consult the Information Centre.

To get to the start of the walk, drive 6,6 km from the Nature Reserve's entrance gate to the signposted turn-off left to Bordjiesrif. Some 1,2 km down this road a tarred road branches left to Venus Pool; it is not signposted. About 250 m along this road, it reaches to the top of a small rise before dropping to the coast; the path to Kanonkop starts here. The path first rises fairly steeply up the slope before it swings right along the contour and heads up the southern flank of a low, broad valley. (This section of the route follows a game trail to the head of the valley.) Here the path swings north-east to cross an old track and, in the rocks above the track, east along the ridge to the cannon. Along the route, the vegetation is low fynbos; in early summer, the veld is splashed white by plants of the everlasting *Helichrysum vestitum*, a spectacular sight when in full flower. From the rocky outcrop on which the cannon rests there are views of Buffelsbaai and the Vasco da Gama

Monument, with Cape Point in the distance. To the north is Paulsberg with its sheer eastern cliffs, characteristic of the peaks on this coast. The walk from the start to Kanonkop takes approximately 40 minutes.

The return route starts down a small gully just to the south of the ridge on which the cannon rests. On the flat area just above the gully there is a curious collection of rocks; one of these has the appearance of a doleful man and is known as Mr Smith; next to him there is an uncharacteristically (for Table Mountain sandstone) hemispherical rock which is covered with bright red lichen. The return path drops down the gully at an increasing gradient until it swings right under a small rocky bluff and heads south to drop into a small kloof which leads shortly to the Venus Pool road next to the sea. This little kloof is unique in the reserve as it contains vestiges of Afromontane forest. Turn right along the tarred road. A short way along the road on

The everlasting Helichrysum vestitum *transforms the veld at Cape Point when it flowers in early summer.*

CHACMA BABOONS

Of all the larger animals which once roamed the Peninsula, the Chacma baboons (*Papio ursinus*) have best withstood the effects wrought by man on their environment. One of the reasons for their survival is the intelligence and adaptability of baboons. Another is that baboons are omnivorous, in nature eating a wide variety of insects, bulbs, roots, flowers and fruit and even, on occasion, small animals. In the Cape of Good Hope Nature Reserve troops of baboons have adapted to feeding on shellfish along the coast as well. Unfortunately, baboons have also learnt that humans are a source of food because they scavenge dustbins and are also fed by people who derive great entertainment from watching their antics. The feeding of baboons is, in fact, a crime, not a joke, and carries stiff penalties. The reason is that baboons become accustomed to hand-outs and when these are no longer forthcoming, they can become aggressive and dangerous. The destruction of these animals may then become necessary to protect the public. Feeding a baboon amounts to signing its death warrant.

Baboons are seldom encountered by walkers outside the Cape of Good Hope Reserve, although they are frequently seen next to the road below Chapman's Peak and above Smitswinkel Bay waiting for hand-outs. In the reserve there are four troops, each with its own exclusive territory. The troops have a strictly hierarchical social structure with the dominant male at the head, defending his position against attacks by younger aspirant males until eventually ousted. The 'pecking order' is followed when feeding, with males eating first, followed by the females and young. Arbitrary hand-outs to individuals low down in the pecking order lead to conflict within the troop and the disturbance of a social system which has evolved as the optimum for these animals.

Baboons are seldom aggressive to walkers but there have been cases of individuals (probably older males ousted from the troop) threatening hikers – but only in order to get at the food they have learnt is to be found in rucksacks. In the unlikely event of a confrontation with baboons, just back off.

the right there is a building of stone: this is a lime kiln which was operated by the real Mr Smith, the farmer-owner of this part of Cape Point before it became a reserve. The low limestone cliffs behind the kiln provided the raw material for the operation, which was one of unusual sophistication; the plans for the kiln and the process were imported from England by Mr Smith. The limestone cliffs are riddled with caves which, as shellfish and other remains indicate, were used by the strandlopers thousands of years before the first European saw this coast. It takes 40 minutes to walk from Kanonkop back to the start. It is quite possible that you may pick up a number of ticks during the course of your walk, so be sure to check your body and clothing thoroughly once you have reached the end.

5.3 COASTAL WALK

A coastal walk from Gifkommetjie to the Cape of Good Hope and a climb to Cape Point

The stretch of Atlantic coastline between Gifkommetjie and Platboom is wild and untouched by man except for the path and the flotsam and jetsam along the high-water mark. From the bay at Platboom a tarred road runs next to the rocks, south to the parking area under the Cape of Good Hope. One of the best-trodden paths on the Peninsula climbs steeply up the Cape and across a shallow nek to the parking area at Cape Point. The route can be conveniently shortened by taking only one or two of these sections. The whole walk really needs a full day as there are so many distractions along the way which need time to be enjoyed.

To reach the parking area at Gifkommetjie, take the turn-off right, sign-posted 'Circular Drive', 5,7 km from the entrance to the reserve along the main road to Cape Point. This road branches, the left-hand branch leading to a cul-de-sac where you can park. Gifkommetjie is so named because of the poisonous plants which grow there: wild ruminants knew to avoid these, but when this area was grazed, stock succumbed.

An obvious path leads from the sea-facing side of the parking area down to the sea. Although it takes only 20 minutes to walk down the path, it traverses two distinct and disjunct veld types: the fynbos of the rocky upper slope gives way to dune thicket dominated by dense wind-clipped milkwood trees (*Sideroxylon inerme*) through which you press before you break out onto the rocks next to the

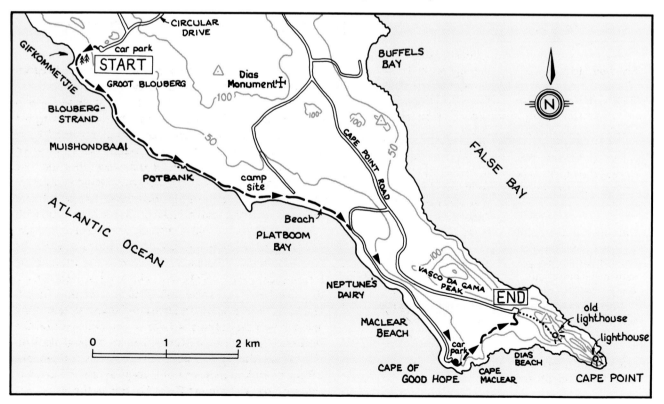

Spring flowers add a dash of colour to the streamlet at Platboom.

Time: 3½-4 hours at a leisurely pace.

Exertion: Light.

Height climbed: 100 m.

Start: The parking area which terminates the Gifkommetjie road off the Circular Drive in the Cape of Good Hope Nature Reserve.

Route summary:
1. A short climb from the start down a fairly steep path to the coast at Gifkommetjie (20 minutes).
2. An easy walk along the beach to Platboom (2-2½ hours).
3. An easy walk along the beach or road from Platboom to the Cape of Good Hope parking area (40 minutes).
4. Initially a steep climb up the Cape of Good Hope followed by an easy climb to the parking area at Cape Point (40 minutes).

Options: This walk can be shortened by starting or finishing at any of the points along the road between Platboom and the Cape of Good Hope parking area.

Difficult terrain: The climb up the Cape of Good Hope is on a very wide path but with steep falls away from the path.

shore. Here you find the characteristic low, matted vegetation resistant to wind and salt spray.

From this point directions are really superfluous; a well-defined path runs left (south) along the coast, skirting the rocks next to the shore on which walking can be time-consuming. This path becomes a track midway between Gifkommetjie and Platboom. It would require enormous self-control not to stray from the path, however, as there are pools with bright red sea-anemones, strange red- and orange-brown rocks extending into the sea, small bays with the kelp lying stark against the sand, shells in profusion and birds, birds, birds. Groups of gulls, sunbathing on the rocks, lift at your approach and hover in the wind before settling again. A pair of Oystercatchers stay at a respectable distance from you as you follow them until they fly off. Flocks of Terns take off and twist and dive before settling again as you pass. Skeins of Cape Cormorants pass on the horizon; if you are lucky, you may disturb a large flock on the sea, and the sky will darken as thousands of them take off together. You may, as I did, come across the unusual sight of a pair of Egyptian Geese floating in the waves past

TOP LEFT: *The rare* Staavia dodii *grows only at Cape Point.* BELOW LEFT: *A Whitebreasted Cormorant.* CENTRE: *Cape Cormorants flock above the strangely coloured rocks near Gifkommetjie.*

a rock with its contingent of cormorants. Kiewiets explode unexpectedly from the short grass and scream at you for coming too close. You are treated to a feast of colour by the orange lichens on the boulders competing with that unique green of a clear cold sea running over white sands as the rollers continue to pour in. If you marched down this section of the route, I suppose you could cover it in an hour or so; rather allow at least 2 hours, not counting stops.

Platboom probably refers to the wind-clipped appearance of the milkwoods here. At Platboom there is a wide sandy bay enjoyed by surfers, with access from a tarred road which leads off the main Cape Point road and runs along

the south arm of the bay along the coast to the Cape of Good Hope. The path and road coincide in places where the rocks come close to the road, as at Neptune's Dairy, a small, rocky bay on the way. The parking bay at the Cape of Good Hope is situated under its sheer cliffs which lie on a resistant bed of granite against which the waves smash, sending spray shooting 15 m into the air. The Cape of Good Hope marks the southern tip of the Peninsula. It takes only 40 minutes to walk from Platboom to the parking area here.

From the parking area, there is an obvious path which climbs straight up the steep slope to the nek between the twin peaklets of the Cape. Although the path is wide and safe, there are sheer drops from it in places and you should be careful if a strong wind is blowing. From the nek the path drops down and runs roughly east above the sheer rocky drop to Dias Beach below, before climbing the slope

to the parking bay at Cape Point. Wooden steps have been constructed to provide access off this path down to Dias Beach. From the parking area below the Cape of Good Hope to that of Cape Point is a 40-minute walk.

The lighthouse on top of Cape Point, a familiar landmark, no longer functions. Because cloud often covers the peak and makes it difficult to see, it was replaced by a new lighthouse only 70 m above the sea on the southern cliff face after the liner *Lusitania* was wrecked here in 1911. It is worth the short walk to the old lighthouse from the parking area for the views from here.

This coast is notoriously windy. It is more comfortable to walk with the wind at your back; reverse the route if the south-easter is blowing. Be careful if a strong wind is blowing through the nek on the Cape of Good Hope; it can knock you off your feet.

BIBLIOGRAPHY

Adamson, R.S. and Salter, T.M., *Flora of the Cape Peninsula*, Juta, Cape Town and Johannesburg, 1950.

Anon., *Table Mountain Guide*, Cape Town Section of the Mountain Club of South Africa, Cape Town, 1952.

Banks, C.H., 'The Lister Nursery', *Veld and Flora*, 61(1), 30-31, June 1975.

Brossy, Shirley, *A Walking Guide for the Hout Bay to Simon's Town Mountains*, published by the author, 1989.

Brossy, Shirley, *A Walking Guide for Table Mountain,* published by the author, 1988.

Bulpin, T.V., *Discovering Southern Africa*, T.V. Bulpin Publications, Cape Town, 1980.

Burman, Jose, *Latest Walks in the Cape Peninsula*, Human & Rousseau, Cape Town and Pretoria, 1979.

Claassen, A.J.M. and Dickson, C.G.C., *Butterflies of the Table Mountain Range*, Struik, Cape Town, 1980.

De Beer, Mona, *The Lion Mountain and the Story of Bantry Bay, Clifton and Camps Bay on the Atlantic Coast of the Cape Peninsula*, A.A. Balkema, Cape Town/Rotterdam, 1987.

Griffiths, Charles L., 'Lichens – Remarkable Plant Partnerships', *Saggitarius*, 5(1), 24-26, 1990.

Hey, D., *Cape of Good Hope Nature Reserve*, Cape Province Department of Nature and Environmental Conservation.

Jackson, W.P.U., *Wild Flowers of Table Mountain*, Howard Timmins, Cape Town, 1982.

Kench, John, *Know Table Mountain*, Chameleon Press, Diep River, 1988.

Kidd, Mary Maytham, *Cape Peninsula – South African Wild Flower Guide 3*, Botanical Society of South Africa, Claremont, 1983.

Luckhoff, C.A., *Table Mountain – History, Flora, Mountain-eering, Conservation – Our National Heritage after Three Hundred Years*, A.A. Balkema, Cape Town, 1951.

McMahon, Liz and Fraser, Michael, *A Fynbos Year*, David Philip, Cape Town and Johannesburg, 1988.

Moll, E.J. and Campbell, B.M., *The Ecological Status of Table Mountain*, Department of Botany, University of Cape Town, Rondebosch, 1976.

Moll, Eugene, and Scott, Lindsay, *Trees and Shrubs of the Cape Peninsula*, Department of Botany, University of Cape Town, Rondebosch, 1981.

Moll, Glen, *Table Mountain – A Natural Wonder*, The Wildlife Society of Southern Africa, Kirstenhof, 1987.

Odden, Eddie and Lee, Nick, *Cape Point*, Don Nelson, Cape Town, n.d.

Richardson, D.M., *Plant Invaders. Hakea species – Hakea sericea, H. gibbosa, H. suaveolens*, Department of Environment Affairs, Pretoria, 1989.

Rourke, J.P., *The Proteas of Southern Africa*, Purnell, Cape Town, Johannesburg and London, 1980.

Robinson, A.M.L. (ed) *The Letters of Lady Anne Barnard*, A.A. Balkema, Cape Town, 1973.

Stewart, Joyce, Linder, H.P., Schelpe, E.A. and Hall, A.V., *Wild Orchids of Southern Africa*, Macmillan South Africa, Johannesburg, 1982.

Williams, Ion J.M., *A Revision of the Genus Leucadendron (Proteaceae)*, Bolus Herbarium, University of Cape Town, Rondebosch, 1972.

Wilson, P.A.S., *A Leaf Key to 45 Common Trees of Table Mountain*, Directorate of Forestry and Environmental Conservation, Department of Water Affairs, Forestry and Environmental Conservation, Pretoria, 1981.

INDEX

Please note: Main reference to walks are in **bold.** References to illustrations are in *italics.*